W9-BOA-246

Government
Support
for Exports

Government Support for Exports

A Second-Best Alternative

Penelope Hartland-Thunberg
Morris H. Crawford

Foreword by
Senator William V. Roth, Jr.

A Report of the U.S. Export
Competitiveness Project,
The Center for Strategic
and International Studies,
Georgetown University

LexingtonBooks
D.C. Heath and Company
Lexington, Massachusetts
Toronto

Library of Congress Cataloging in Publication Data

Hartland-Thunberg, Penelope.
  Government support for exports.

  "A report of the U.S. Export Competitiveness Project, the Center for Strategic and International Studies, Georgetown University."
  Includes bibliographical references and index.
  1. United States—Commercial policy. 2. Export credit—United States. I. Crawford, Morris H. II. U.S. Export Competitiveness Project. III. Title.
HF1455.H35   382'.63'0973   82–7732
ISBN 0–669–05692–8   AACR2

Contents

List of Tables

About the U.S. Export Competitiveness Project

The U.S. share of the world export market is in a serious long-term decline. From a 28 percent share of foreign markets in 1962, the United States dropped to nearly 20 percent in 1980. There are several reasons for this market decline: excessive export controls, financial and legal constraints, and active promotion by our competitors, conditions that are especially apparent in U.S. trade relations with the Third World. Not enough has been done to understand and correct this trend and to stimulate the exports that would help reverse the U.S. balance-of-trade deficit.

It is increasingly clear that in the 1980s the United States should reexamine its antiquated export-promotion policies. The stakes are high. Failure to expand exports will erode U.S. economic, strategic, and political positions in the world. Because the issue is moving to a central position in national political debate, the Center for Strategic and International Studies has undertaken a project on the competitiveness of U.S. exports. The purpose of the project is to encourage a greater understanding by decision makers and the public of the issue and to provide policy recommendations to meet the demands placed on American business in overseas competition.

This examination of government support for exports—a second-best alternative—is an important addition to the books already published by CSIS as a result of the research undertaken by the project. The Center shares the authors' expectations that their findings will have a direct relevance to the decisions that are to be made and that public concern for the direction of policy on U.S. exports will be stimulated.

David M. Abshire
Chairman, The Center for Strategic and
International Studies

Foreword

The United States faces serious challenges in the international marketplace at a level virtually unmatched in recent history. Our merchandise trade deficits continue to grow, reaching $28 billion on a balance-of-payments basis in 1981. Our market share in goods trade at home and abroad has been seriously eroded by competition from the European Community, Japan, and the newly industrializing countries around the rim of Asia and Latin America; and although strong at the present time, U.S. service industries fear they will soon see markets overrun by tough foreign competitors.

A portion of this competition results from the growth and increasing sophistication of trading partners, like Japan, which possess some of the most modern and efficient plant and equipment in the world. Some of this competition also comes from foreign industries that have been developed to serve a world, rather than merely a domestic market, thereby achieving substantial economies of scale. Most troublesome, however, is the growing use of unfair trade practices by countries attempting to capture an undue share of world markets. Such beggar-thy-neighbor practices unjustly deny the United States expanded export and job opportunities.

For years the United States has carried the free-trade banner, believing that an open U.S. market will mean lower prices and greater consumer choice at home and equivalent open-market opportunities abroad. We have initiated successive rounds of multilateral trade negotiations under the General Agreement on Tariffs and Trade (GATT), reducing U.S. tariffs and opening our borders with the expectation that other countries would follow our lead.

We have not, however, been successful in our pursuit of free and fair trade worldwide. Even though, in fact, the Tokyo Round of negotiations reduced average developed-country tariffs to 3 or 4 percent, foreign markets are far from open, and trade continues to be constrained by government actions. These actions, aimed at the achievement of domestic economic objectives, serve to prevent the United States and other competitors from gaining an equitable share of the global purchasing pie.

One of the most distortive examples of government involvement in trade is the use of subsidies designed to capture foreign markets. Direct-export subsidies, such as those provided by the European Community to spur overseas sales of agricultural products, have displaced U.S. producers in third markets, leading to job losses at home. Officially supported export credits—the focus of this study—have crippled U.S. efforts to compete fairly for contracts on a wide range of products. Such government interventions in the marketplace seriously tinker with the laws of comparative advantage. Moreover, they force the United States to respond in kind, retaliate, or risk losing markets and bases for continued production of many goods, including those in the vital high-technology sector.

As in GATT-covered trade barriers, the United States has attempted to eliminate officially supported credits by convincing our trading partners of the long-term costs and deleterious effects of their use. Our efforts in the Organization for Economic Cooperation and Development (OECD) have been to no avail, however. Countries like France continue to support nearly 30 percent of their exports with official credits set at artificially low rates.

In a perfect world of free trade based on the market mechanism, I would not want to see the United States provide subsidized export credits. Ours is not a perfect world, however, and the United States can no longer afford to base its policy and program priorities on the notion that other countries will eventually compete fairly. In today's reality, subsidies afforded by our trading partners threaten our world position and overall job stability and must be dealt with strongly.

In this light, Penelope Hartland-Thunberg's and Morris Crawford's study is a timely, incisive, and valuable contribution to discussions on the future of U.S. export activities. The authors provide important insights into the effects of foreign-government support for exports and, most importantly, make useful suggestions on the means of best meeting the competition. Their recommendations are worth careful study and should assist policymakers and the public in fashioning the optimal approach to achieving export preeminence once again.

Exports can be America's engine of growth and can bring us through the 1980s and into the 1990s with a strong economy. We must take actions, now, however, if we hope to achieve our long-range international economic goals.

Senator William V. Roth, Jr.

Preface

The United States appears to be moving along in the 1980s with a highly ambivalent export policy. On the one hand, U.S. exporters are to be encouraged, if the Reagan administration has its way, by a variety of measures, some of which would remove existing governmental obstacles to exports (in the form of inflexible or counterproductive government regulations) while others would create new vehicles to facilitate exports (for example, export trading companies). On the other hand, slashing of the lending authority of the Export-Import Bank of the United States (Eximbank), an institution that for half a century has helped to finance U.S. exports, would emasculate an export-support program at a time when foreign competition facing U.S. export industries is becoming more intense than ever before in the postwar era.

Similar ambiguities are evident in Washington's behavior toward research and development (R&D). High-technology industries and exports require continued replenishment from ongoing R&D. While we seem to be losing ground in technological competition with Japan and Western Europe, the administration has cut back our spending for basic research that is essential to the nation's long-term technological strength. It has shown little inclination, moreover, to commit the nation to technological leadership and to all-out technological competitiveness in world trade.

The internal inconsistencies in the emerging U.S. export policy seem to stem from inadequate attention to the nature of the structural imbalances in the world economy and their implications for the future of world trade. They seem also to stem from an overly doctrinaire application of economic theory to circumstances where that theory does not apply.

Why should the United States, or any other country, be concerned with exports? Exports are in the public interest for two basic reasons: to make imports possible and to maximize the productivity of a country's resources. The first reason is self-evident; the second stems from the first. To consume at reasonable prices goods we do not produce in sufficient quantity (ranging from bananas to petroleum), we export goods we can produce at a reasonable price. The key word is *reasonable*. We could grow bananas in a hothouse, but they would be prohibitively expensive compared with imports. We can produce gasoline from coal but even at today's astronomic prices for Organization of Petroleum Exporting Countries (OPEC) oil, the cost of the synthetic is still more expensive.

By using labor and machinery to produce for export agricultural produce and capital goods (at which we are very efficient) and thus pay for our imports, the total volume of goods and services that U.S. consumers value highly is far greater than would be the case if we were to prohibit imports. Exporting those goods we produce most efficiently permits a larger volume of output from the same amount of inputs and thus a higher level of productivity for each unit of labor and capital used in production. This exchange of exports for imports in turn makes possible a higher level of gross national product (GNP) and means that an average dollar's worth of exports adds more to GNP than an average dollar's worth of production for domestic consumption. Thus statements such as that of a high Treasury Department official that "a dollar's worth of exports adds no more to GNP than a dollar's worth of production for domestic consumption" contain sloppy thinking and are in fact a misstatement.[1]

There is one important qualification to the productivity benefits from exports. The enhanced productivity of a country's resources occurs only provided the basic competitive forces of supply and demand are allowed to operate in the world economy without distortions from government interference or monopolistic control. If the market is allowed to determine which industries are to be export industries and which are to be import-competing industries, productivity will be maximized. In a world of really free trade, export subsidies (with one exception discussed below) would lower the availability of the goods and services a country's population values most highly and thus would not be in the national interest. Such, unfortunately, is not the world in which we live.

Other governments do subsidize their exports; the free-trade argument against export subsidies by the United States consequently is not applicable today. In this book we address the question of proper U.S. policy toward export subsidies in the world of the 1980s—*proper policy* meaning that policy that will maximize the productivity of U.S. resources in a world of considerable government interference with the free-market mechanism.

We first examine the evolving role of the United States in world markets in the context of the conditions in which government interference with the free flow of foreign trade in the form of export subsidies is justified in the national interest (as opposed to narrow sectional interests). This discussion explores two bases for such government interference, one on economic grounds and the other on national-security grounds. We then examine alternative forms of government support for U.S. exports and the choice among them in terms of economic rationale and political feasibility. The discussion concentrates on exports of manufactured goods; it excludes consideration of the special problems associated with exports of agricultural commodities.

The term *goods* as used in this study includes both commodities and services. There is convincing evidence, despite inadequate statistical collections, that the United States has a strong comparative advantage in the production of such services as computer software, data communications, industrial design, and some aspects of finance and engineering. It is essential in a study related to export competitiveness to include services trade even though the full range of service items in which the United States has a comparative advantage will not be clear until the application of the concept to services industries in general has been more fully explored and more data have been collected and analyzed.

We conclude that the national interests of the United States would best be served by an elimination of export subsidies worldwide. Barring the best solution, however, the second-best choice calls for export subsidies sufficient to permit most U.S. exporters to meet subsidized foreign competition. The second-best solution would produce a level and industrial composition of income and employment in the United States closest to the best solution but not as high. The net costs are lowest and the potential benefits are highest with the second-best alternative provided only that the first choice is not within the reach of the United States.

Acknowledgments

The debts I have accumulated in the course of writing this book are vast. The initiation of the project depended crucially on the insights and energies of Michael A. Samuels, formerly executive director of Third World Studies at the Center for Strategic and International Studies; financial support was provided by the U.S. Export Competitiveness Project that has been underway at the Center since 1979. Morris Crawford, president of International Informatics Consultants, was the principal drafter of chapter 3 on research and development; in addition he read and offered encouragement, as well as valuable comments, on the entire manuscript.

Many other people in the public and private sectors contributed their time and intellectual energies to a detailed discussion of the ideas contained in the draft of this book, so many, in fact, that an attempt to cite them all is impractical. Without their aid, however, this study would have been incomplete. Any errors or omissions of events occurring before the end of 1981 are my responsibility.

Penelope Hartland-Thunberg

1 The Reasons for Export Subsidies

Government support for exports, including export financing, can take many forms, all of which amount to direct or indirect subsidies. Subsidies for exports are justified on one or both of two grounds: for economic reasons and for national-security reasons. Not all export items can be justified for government subsidies by either of these reasons; government subsidies for some export items are justified by one or both of these grounds.

Economic Reasons

In an ideal world where all transactions are governed by market forces and competition, with no government interference, administered prices, or monopolistic control, there would be an economic justification for export subsidies solely in the so-called infant-industry argument. In such a case a government could improve the future economic well-being of the country by temporarily subsidizing the exports of a newly established industry while it is still relatively high cost, compared to foreign competitors, because of lack of experience and a limited domestic market. Given adequate management and a labor force capable of acquiring the necessary skills within a foreseeable time span, the industry would be likely to reach maturity (that is, attain costs as low as those of its older, established competitors abroad) within the span of a decade or so. Upon maturity the subsidy would be discontinued. As a consequence of the period of government support, the industrial structure of a country's comparative advantage would have been altered in such a way as to have lifted the productivity of its capital and labor in the recently established industry. Gross national product (GNP) and average per-capita income would be permanently raised to a new, higher level than would have been true without the subsidy, especially if there had previously been extensive unemployment in the country.

The infant-industry argument for subsidies obviously applies only to countries with a small domestic market attempting to restructure their economies by initiating and competing with technologies already being employed elsewhere in the world. As a technological leader in the world and, in addition, possessed of the world's largest domestic market, the

1

United States since World War II has not had occasion to resort to export subsidies to nurture infant industries.[1] The argument is indirectly relevant to the United States, however, because a number of its competitors in the world marketplace are basing their current export policies on the use of subsidies to catch up or overtake the U.S. technological lead in those industries where this country in the past successfully established new growth industries to exploit technological innovations primarily initiated in the United States.

The Foundation for U.S. Export Competitiveness

The history of the U.S. economy and its participation in world trade since World War II has been marked by the emergence of a series of technologically based growth industries that have become its leading export sectors. In a very real sense the dynamics powering the U.S. economy and the world economy have been founded in rapid technological change, in research, much of it begun during World War II, and in the spread and application of research results to an enormous variety of civilian uses. Truly revolutionary changes have been wrought in such industries as transportation, communications, materials processing, construction, and agriculture. A stream of new products emerged that were marketed first at home and then abroad. The growth industries, being highly profitable in the context of what appeared to be limitless markets, inevitably called forth replication abroad. The new foreign competitors, increasingly established with government support in the form of tariff protection or hidden or overt subsidies, supplied an increasing share of the world market (often including the market in the United States as well as in third countries) that originally had been supplied solely from the United States.[2]

A considerable body of economic research supports the concept of such a product cycle that involves research, technological innovation, development, marketing first domestically then in foreign markets, the emergence of competitors, and the eventual decline in market shares of the originator.[3] Examples come quickly to mind. Radio, television, telecommunications, and aerospace are industries whose locus has spread from the country of technological origin around the world or to certain other industrial or industrializing economies. In most cases the geographic dispersion was government sponsored by such encouraging policies as protective tariffs, liberal tax, credit, and depreciation policies, or direct subsidies to research and production.

To some unknown degree the replication abroad of U.S.-based R&D would have occurred eventually without government subsidies. It would have occurred slowly, however, and the stream of export earnings flowing to the U.S. originator would have been more prolonged and larger than in fact it was. The existence of foreign-government subsidies, moreover, whether direct or indirect, undoubtedly produced more investment worldwide in this particular growth industry than would otherwise have taken place and thus smaller profits to many, if not all, participants in this industry.[4]

The replication abroad of new U.S.-based growth industries in many cases was the consequence of the initiatives of the U.S. industry itself. For a variety of reasons—to overcome a high foreign-tariff wall, to take advantage of lower costs of production abroad (resulting from lower foreign wages combined with relatively high productivity, although the lower wages were not infrequently traceable at least in part to an overvalued dollar), to improve their competitive position worldwide, to benefit from lower foreign taxes, more-liberal depreciation policies, or subsidies to the industry offered by foreign governments at the local or national level—U.S. firms established foreign subsidiaries, participated in joint ventures with foreign companies, or licensed foreign firms to produce their product outside the United States.

In most cases the movement of U.S. industry was generated by government policies abroad more favorable than those in the United States.[5] In both cause and effect, the replication abroad of U.S.-based growth industries through either U.S. or foreign initiative is thus the same. The investment in the industry abroad occurred sooner and in greater volume than it would have had the market mechanism not been altered by foreign-government policy. More important, at least during periods of full employment, resources in the United States were diverted away from export industries toward domestic industries of lower productivity as a consequence of foreign subsidies.

Productivity in export industries is higher on the average than productivity in domestic industries because in open, competitive world markets, the most efficient (most productive) industries are the only successful export industries. Their greater efficiency and higher productivity in international comparisons will be based on some cost advantage over their foreign competitors. This cost advantage may be the result of nature's bounty, the special skills of its work force or management, its large accumulation of capital, the innovativeness of its scientists, or other similar favorable circumstances. It is important to note that in international comparisons of productivity (and comparative advantage), what is being compared is not solely the technical capacity to produce but also market values. Productivity is related to the value the marketplace puts on the product or the service as well as to the technical capacity to turn it out in maximum volume with a minimum of inputs. The technical capacity to produce a new widget has no economic significance if society is not willing to spend money on this widget. The more money the world is willing to spend on their widget, the more productive are the inputs used in producing it (the higher is the value of their combined effort).

In those cases when the replication of U.S.-based growth industries was stimulated by lower foreign costs of production *not* the consequence of government policy, the flow of resources into the industry abroad was a response to the market mechanism and in that sense not a misallocation from the U.S. viewpoint. Such cases are to be found primarily in direct foreign investment in the less-developed countries (LDCs). The production there in affiliates of U.S. manufacturing concerns of labor-intensive components is frequently, however, also encouraged by LDC tax policies that favor foreign investment. Taiwan and Korea are prime examples.

As long as the U.S. economy was technologically vibrant, generating a broad and deep flow of new products and services, the appearance of subsidized foreign competition and the consequent foreshortening of the stream of earnings from the exports of any one new product was not a source of urgent national concern. This was true because the export-earnings stream was constantly replenished in depth by the appearance of yet another new export item. Similarly the impact on U.S. productivity of the diversion of resources from U.S. growth industries was in part compensated by the flow of resources into newer growth industries as they emerged. The early appearance of new competitors or the appearance of an excessive number of new competitors served to prevent an appreciation of the dollar's exchange rate or to slow the accumulation of foreign exchange by the U.S. banking system. Internally it diminished employment opportunities in some localities sooner and to a greater degree than would otherwise have happened, but the development of new products often occurred in the vicinity of the maturing (less rapidly growing) older industries, and the disruption was not acute for the total economy.[6] This is in no way meant to belittle the all-too-often very painful consequent disruption to individuals and to firms. In the past, however, the necessary adjustments were highly localized geographically and industrially and could be managed as such. Today dangers of disruption are national in scope and should be managed as such; a worldwide misallocation of resources is being accelerated in directions and to a degree that threatens U.S. national interests.

The Challenge of the 1980s and Beyond

Economic history will judge the decade of the 1970s as revolutionary. Two dramatic reversals occurred in the early years of the decade, either one of which by itself was capable of altering fundamental relations between national economies and the operation of the world market. In 1972–1973 the world shifted from a regime of fixed exchange rates to one of managed but fluctuating rates, and the dollar was depreciated. In 1973–1974 the price of oil was wrenched violently upward by a precipitous rise of 400 percent when the control of oil prices shifted from the Gulf of Mexico to the Persian Gulf. Then at the end of the decade the new higher price level was again abruptly tripled.

The depreciation of the dollar meant that some U.S. industries for which exports were not profitable at the old rate now could profitably engage in exports. It also meant that some U.S. industries that had been seriously hit by import competition now could compete with imports in their home market more successfully. The list for the United States of market-determined export industries was lengthened, that of import-competing industries was shortened. Turkish towels and television sets, for example, are now being exported, and bicycles are once again being produced in the United States. By this currency change the extent of U.S. comparative advantage in the world market had been deepened; that of countries whose currencies were appreciated vis-a-vis the dollar had been made more shallow.

At the same time the advent of fluctuating dollar exchange rates brought an end to the era of gradual appreciation of the dollar, with its consequent shrinking of the list of industries in which the United States possessed a comparative advantage. Fluctuating exchange rates imply an ebb and flow at the margin of market-determined export industries. Thus, during those intervals when the dollar is appreciating, U.S. exports will decline and U.S. imports will rise, although the effects will not be observable in trade flows until after a year to eighteen months. The current strength of the dollar foreshadows a deterioration of the U.S. trade balance in 1982.[7]

Although the regime of fluctuating exchange rates has caused the list of U.S. export industries to expand and contract at the margin, the quantum jump in oil prices in addition altered the intramarginal structure of comparative-advantage positions among world trading partners and by itself set in motion forces that will further alter the industrial pattern of comparative advantage for all parts of the world economy. Energy is so pervasive an input into all industries and so essential to the productive process that it can quite properly be viewed as a basic factor of production. The existing structure of national comparative-advantage positions around the world has been altered because comparative advantage is determined by relative prices of basic factors of production. The quadrupling in the price of oil meant that one of the cheapest factors of production now became the most expensive. Energy-intensive industries around the world have become less profitable, and those economies most dependent on energy-intensive industries are most seriously affected.

The impact of the shift in relative prices on patterns of comparative advantage is of fundamental long-term importance to the United States and the rest of the trading world. It is still in train. It will not be complete until shifts in demand and supply for nearly all goods and services produced—these shifts having been generated by the change in the relative price of energy—have worked through the world system. The supply shifts may require many years to implement because higher energy prices set in motion research on new sources of energy and new ways of conserving on energy that is likely to generate new industries and make existing industries obsolete. The impetus behind this search was given added strength by the tripling of oil prices in 1979–1980.

The first country to achieve a technological breakthrough in energy conservation or replacement and to develop it is likely to be the prime growth economy of the future. The world will beat a path to its door. Its balance-of-payments problems and export expansion problems will be solved for some years. In terms of experience, Europe may be better positioned than the United States to achieve such a breakthrough because in the past, while U.S. technology has been oriented toward labor-saving devices (labor having been the expensive input in the United States), European technology has been oriented toward energy and materials-saving research. Because of much higher petroleum taxes, energy was relatively more expensive in Europe than in the United States.

Meanwhile, however, more marginal shifts in energy conservation are being implemented around the world supplemented by government policies aimed at a restructuring of national economies. Oil-importing countries, suffering oil-induced balance-of-payments deficits and inflation, are keenly aware of the need for such restructuring. Japan and several European countries, whose economies are much more dependent on imported oil and export markets than that of the United States, are systematically adjusting government programs to encourage exports to pay for oil imports and to help maintain domestic employment that is being curtailed by anti-inflationary monetary policies. Their reindustrialization programs are aimed at exports and look to the United States as a model for new growth opportunities. They are seeking to replicate U.S. growth industries; aerospace, telecommunications, and semiconductors, for example, are benefiting from government support in Europe, Japan, or both.[8]

During the postwar period Japan and Europe frequently looked to the United States for new growth industries when they sought to improve the structure of their comparative advantage. In the 1980s, however, structural readjustments will be pursued more vigorously and more simultaneously than ever before because of the pressure of the oil-induced balance-of-payments deficits, inflationary price rises, and shifting cost-price relations.

In the 1930s, keen competition in international trade took the form of competitive currency depreciations. If one country makes its currency cheaper in terms of other currencies, its exports will be stimulated and its imports retarded because of the resulting price changes. If, however, all countries attempt the same strategy, no one benefits more than temporarily, and if competitive depreciation is combined with higher import barriers, as it was in the 1930s, everyone suffers.

The 1980s appear to be witnessing a more-sophisticated version of the beggar-thy-neighbor depreciation strategy of the 1930s. The effects of currency depreciation—lowering the price of one country's exports to foreign purchasers and raising the price of that country's imports to its own citizens—can be achieved through a variety of measures. Subsidies to exports will permit exportables to be sold abroad more cheaply; taxes, quotas, administrative delays, and red tape can limit imports and make them more expensive. The combination has the same effect as a partial currency depreciation limited to certain commodity trade transactions. If the country is an international borrower, the combination has an advantage over straightforward currency depreciation in that it would not make more burdensome the interest and amortization charges on its foreign debt.

The upswing of protectionist practices by various members of the European Economic Community (EEC) is unprecedented in that it is aimed at imports from fellow EEC members as well as outsiders. At the same time, aid to industries engaged in exports has become more liberal. Government-aided export credits have become so generous the *Economist* (London) was led recently to declare that economic warfare has broken out in the export-credit field. For years the Japanese government has directed the industrial structure of its economy and its exports through various credit, financial, tax, and import policies.[9]

Subjected to a concerted competitive drive by most industrialized and industrializing countries simultaneously, the United States is experiencing competitive pressures in world markets more intense than in the usual cyclical downswing because it is not usual for all countries to go into recession at the same time. The more-intense world competition challenging the United States in the 1980s would stretch the country's public and private entrepreneurial capacities even if the stream of new products flowing from American laboratories and workshops were as heavy and deep as twenty years ago.[10] Available evidence suggests that technological innovation in the United States is slowing, especially in relation to such activity abroad.[11] If the stream of new products becoming available for marketing abroad is indeed thinning, then the artificial foreshortening of the stream of U.S. export earning, which is the consequence of foreign-export subsidies, will be less and less covered over by the creation of additional new earnings streams. Similarly, the boost to productivity from the emergence of new growth industries will less and less compensate for the diversion of resources away from existing growth industries as a result of foreign subsidies. To the degree that U.S. technological growth is slowing, the future role of the United States in the world economy appears troubled.

The Second Best

In such a situation, where does the U.S. national interest lie? What policy posture is optimum for the United States? Economics has a ready answer: elimination of all government subsidies and other interferences with competition and the market mechanism would be in the best interest of the United States and at least some of the other subsidizing countries. If, however, the rest of the world refuses to behave in this fashion, as it has so far, what is the second-best course for the United States? Economics does not have a ready answer for questions relating to second-best options: the answer depends on the specifics of the situation. The theory of the second best, however, does tell us unequivocally that if the conditions necessary for the best solution do not exist, the second-best solution does not necessarily require the existence of those same conditions and indeed may require removal of those same conditions.[12]

The point is important because both the Reagan administration and the Congressional Budget Office (CBO) justify cutting government support for export credit financing using what is essentially the free-trade argument.[13] It is true that in most cases a nation would worsen its own economic position if it introduced export subsidies in a world of free competitive markets. The United States in the 1980s, however, faces a world containing many government subsidies to exports and a widening variety of nontariff barriers to imports—in general many constraints to free competition. The best solution—elimination of all government interference in trade—is not currently available to the United States. The second-best solution for the United States does not necessarily require that it practice a free-trade policy (when its trading partners do not) to make the best of a second-best alternative. In fact, the second-best solution may require at least a partial abandonment of a free-trade policy.

The specifics of the United States in the world economy of the 1980s strongly suggest that the second-best policy for the nation is to counter foreign subsidies sufficiently to neutralize them as far as possible in industries in which the United States has a clear comparative advantage.[14] The United States by itself can do nothing about the subsidy-induced overinvestment worldwide in the industries concerned, but it can counter somewhat the distortion of geographic patterns of trade by matching competitors' subsidies. With such a policy the volume of U.S. exports and the stream of U.S. export earnings over the full period of the product's life would be larger (and thus the diminution of U.S. productivity smaller) than if the United States did not meet the competition, but not so large as it would have been in a purely competitive world.

As the CBO pointed out, if the economy were fully employed with no excess capacity, such a policy of export subsidies would divert resources from domestic to international markets. In fact such a subsidy would divert U.S. resources back toward the pattern that would have existed if there were no foreign government subsidies. With no interference, the world market mechanism would have resulted in a higher level of U.S. exports than has actually been the case. Whether the United States will, in fact, attain full employment in the near term is controversial. If, however, it is achieved, a diversion of U.S. resources away from the domestic market to foreign markets would still be necessary because more U.S. goods must be exported to pay for higher-priced oil imports. The subsidies, that is, in either case would be working with market forces, not against them as the foreign subsidies do; they would serve to maintain the level of resources employed in our most-efficient and hence most-productive industries.

Subsidies represent a budget expenditure, the cost of which would be balanced to some degree in the case of the United States in the 1980s, because they would make possible a larger stream of export earnings into the future and a higher level of real income in the United States than would be possible without the subsidies. The impact on the U.S. budget must thus measure the benefit of a higher tax base and lower welfare expenditures, as well as the cost of the subsidy. This benefit flows from the nature of U.S. exports.

The manufactured goods exported by the United States are predominantly either goods embodying new or advanced technology, or if U.S. technology is not more advanced than that of its main competitors, then capital goods often embodied in entire systems—a turnkey plant, a power system, or a telecommunications system, for example. The exports of such systems, the so-called big-ticket items, are similar in their effects to exports of advanced technology in that in most cases they too produce a stream of future U.S. export earnings from the sale of parts and replacements. Similarly the loss by the United States to foreign subsidized competition represents a loss of a future income stream as well as a loss of present export earnings. In the case of exports of civilian aircraft, the value of the future earnings stream stretching out over the next decade is estimated by Boeing to be a multiple of more than three times the value of the export of the system itself.[15]

A benefit of greater basic importance than the budgetary advantage flowing from the neutralizing of foreign subsidies lies in the impact of such a policy on the average level of U.S. productivity. Those countries that lag technologically behind the United States can look to it as a model for proven growth industries in restructuring their economies, but except for a few isolated products, looking elsewhere for a model is not a luxury in which the United States can indulge. The industries in which the United States will be most efficient by 1985 or 1990 can be objectively determined only in the operation of the world market.

Those U.S. industries that prove themselves to be most competitive in meeting existing conditions of world demand and world supply, when neither is manipulated by government interference or monopolistic control, are the country's most-efficient industries. The U.S. manufacturing industries that export the largest share of their output lie primarily in the capital-goods industry—machinery and equipment for manufacturing, transportation, and communication—and especially in those sectors of capital-goods production that are most technologically advanced. In many cases, the R&D costs of these industries are so immense they could never have come into being without the expectation of serving a world market; even the huge domestic U.S. market could not absorb the scale of output necessary to economic operation. A new generation of civilian aircraft today provides an example. By the same token such industries can continue to operate profitably only as long as they are able to serve a world market.

How much more productive is labor and capital when employed in, say, the aerospace industries serving a world market than if employed in making trucks or lathes? There is no foolproof way of measuring the difference. If there were, however, and if the difference should turn out to be marginal, perhaps less than 0.5 percent per year, such a difference could not safely be neglected in a period when declining levels of U.S. productivity are a cause for much concern. Certainly any calculus of the costs and benefits of export subsidies should recognize the existence of such productivity differentials as a benefit, albeit immeasurable. On purely a priori grounds it seems likely that the difference in productivity would be more than marginal.

The range of the productivity benefit to be derived from a policy of neutralizing foreign subsidies can be illustrated by making alternative assumptions about the size of the productivity impact and whether its effect is confined solely to the lost exports or also influences the productivity of the industrial subsector involved (for example, whether the lost productivity is confined solely to the resources not used in exporting civilian aircraft or applies to all the resources employed in firms exporting aircraft). Eximbank credit subsidies is the example chosen, with a direct lending program of $4 billion supporting exports of $6 billion assumed.[16] Table 1-1 illustrates the productivity benefits of a 1 percent and 5 percent productivity differential.

The cost of the Eximbank program, ignoring fees and other earnings (net cash flow loss), depends on the current level of market rates of interest

Table 1-1
Productivity Benefits of Eximbank's Direct-Lending Program
(million dollars)

Productivity Differential	1 Percent	5 Percent
Assuming productivity impact confined to resources directly supported by Eximbank credits	60	300
Assuming productivity impact applies to all resources in industrial subsector[a]	900	4,500

[a]Assuming one-half of the output of the Eximbank-supported industry is affected by Eximbank credits. Thus the table indicates that if the productivity effect of exports amounts to about 1 percent of output and if only the productivity of the labor and capital used in filling Eximbank orders is affected, loss of these orders would cause productivity to decline by $60 million.

in the United States compared with the average rates charged by the bank. Assuming that the latter is 9.0 percent (approximately its current level), the loss for each $1 billion of ten-year loans can be computed for different levels of the rate at which Eximbank borrows (Federal Financing Bank discount rate). If the borrowing rate is 10 percent, the loss to Eximbank of a $4 billion lending program would be $200 million; it would be $600 million at a borrowing rate of 12 percent and $1,200 million at a borrowing rate of 15 percent.

These arithmetic examples do not, of course, prove that productivity benefits are greater than costs or vice-versa. The range of the cost and benefit estimates, however, does suggest that it is not improbable that benefits could exceed costs by a substantial margin. Specifically the assumption that the productivity impact will be confined only to the resources directly supported by Eximbank credits seems much too narrow. In the great majority of cases, the smaller production runs that are the consequence of lost exports would affect adversely the efficiency of the entire operation. In other words, the $900 million estimated productivity impact for a 1 percent differential seems the much more reasonable, although still conservative, figure. The assumption on which it is based—that the productivity of one-half of the output of the Eximbank-supported industry is affected by the bank credits—is probably too conservative for the aerospace industry, although more realistic for the machine tool industry.

Those U.S. export items that involve neither advanced technology nor complete systems represent in a number of cases neither industries of pronounced comparative advantage nor the object of cutthroat competition in other markets. Such industries do not require U.S. government support for purely economic reasons. Government support for such U.S. exports may, however, be justified on national-security grounds. In addition, government support for exports embodying advanced technology or big-ticket items may also be justified on the basis of national-security issues.

A relevant case lies in the export of nuclear-power plants. Present U.S. attitudes do not favor the installation domestically of more such power units, but attitudes abroad differ, and sentiments in the United States could well experience a future change. U.S. access to foreign sources of petroleum is sufficiently precarious that it would be imprudent policy for the United States to deny itself the option of a future turn toward nuclear power. It would be foolhardy to stifle research into improved technologies. The maintenance of an ongoing nuclear-power industry remains in U.S. national-security interests. Subsidies to exports of nuclear-power plants sufficient to meet foreign subsidized competition are a relatively cheap means of maintaining a viable U.S. industry.

National-Security Reasons

That the world has become increasingly interdependent in the last quarter-century is frequently claimed, but the implications of this statement are poorly appreciated. If the boundaries of the concept of national security were originally confined to military matters, they must clearly be broadened to be useful in today's interdependent world. The United States is no longer the master of its own household. The efficient operation of the U.S. economy, for example, was sharply depressed by the oil-price increases abruptly forced on the United States and the oil-consuming world by external events in 1974 and again in 1979. The boosts to both inflation and unemployment in the United States that were the direct consequences of these external events diminished U.S. national security, nearly everyone will agree. On another plane, the clear expansion of world extralegal migration flows and refugee movements will affect the national security of the United States regardless of the policies adopted. Events abroad now influence domestic developments in this country more than in any previous era. To the extent that this has happened, U.S. national security is challenged; our ability to influence events at home as well as abroad is lessened.

A concept or a definition is good only insofar as it is useful. A functional definition of national security would recognize today's heightened interdependencies. National security can be said to reflect the ability of a nation to pursue successfully its national interests as it sees them any place in the world, including at home, using all of the instruments of national policy available to it.[17]

Instruments of national policy can be grouped into four categories:

economic, military, political, and sociocultural. Each instrument of national policy is discrete, but their effects are comprehensive and interrelated. Economic policy has political repercussions at home and abroad, as well as military and social ramifications; military policy has sizable economic, social, and political ramifiations domestically and internationally; political maneuvers in the international arena can bring economic rewards or burdens as well as military and social activity; and sociocultural developments abroad can have substantial military or economic consequences and can induce international political harmony or discord. In brief, the instruments of national policy are all interdependent in their effects; national security is subject to the influence of all, not solely to that of the military instrument.

Once this broadening of the concept of national security is accepted—and to many it is self-evident—certain implications for policy and its implementation follow. The failure since 1973 of U.S. exports to keep pace with imports, despite a series of official U.S. export-promotion programs and the depreciation of the dollar, has been accompanied by a pronounced diminution of U.S. influence in the world arena. To a degree not properly appreciated in this country, U.S. power and prestige in the world arena reflect the relative strength of the U.S. economy. When most of the world wanted to buy U.S. goods because they were the highest in quality and cheapest in price, U.S. power and influence were unsurpassed. In almost any international forum—the United Nations, the General Agreement on Tariffs and Trade (GATT), the International Monetary Fund (IMF), or the World Bank—U.S. initiatives won resounding support. Such is not the case today.

Currency value has traditionally been a symbol of prestige around the world—more so abroad than in the United States. The symbolism of the depreciated dollar, moreover, probably has been exaggerated in foreign perceptions by the fact that the value of the dollar had remained constant at Bretton Woods parities for so long.

The depreciated dollar is viewed as reflecting a failure of the U.S. economy. A diplomat in Bonn was recently cited as saying that the United States would do well to regard its prestige less in terms of military power; he felt this country had never grasped the extent to which the condition of the dollar was a symbol of influence and power and that these had diminished with the dollar's fall.[18]

The dollar, of course, is a symbol of power just because it will be strong only as long as world demand for U.S. goods and services is sustained and growing. Basic to a reestablishment of U.S. power and prestige in the world is a strong, vibrant economy producing a variety of better products. Meanwhile, however, the decline in perceived U.S. economic strength has been accompanied by declining levels of foreign diplomatic acquiescence to U.S.

initiatives. U.S. prestige in the early 1980s is probably lower than it has ever been in this century. Whether justified or not, the denigration of U.S. power has been accompanied by a rising chorus of criticism of U.S. actions and policies by our closest allies and by a new assertiveness on the part of foreigners in regard to U.S. domestic as well as foreign policies. In short, it is not only U.S. economic influence that has waned; U.S. influence in political and military matters has declined as well.

In fact the basic policy differences that have emerged between the United States and its closest allies would have been inconceivable two decades ago, but had they existed, it would have been even more unthinkable that they should result in the kinds of public criticism, contrary initiatives, and constant carping that have been directed at the United States recently. European policy toward the Middle East not only failed to support the Camp David agreements but resulted in a competing European initiative toward that troubled region. European support for U.S. economic sanctions against the Soviet Union after the invasion of Afghanistan was hardly enthusiastic, and even the exquisitely polite Japanese officials have demonstrated an increasing willingness to criticize U.S. policies and actions in recent months. For example, Japan's Prime Minister Zenko Suzuki complained about not having been consulted on the removal of the U.S. partial grain embargo against the Soviet Union.

The diminished political significance of the United States, stemming from its weakened international economic position, has economic repercussions as well. A case in point lies in the report that an important prod to the November 1978 decision to raise U.S. interest rates was the insistence by West Germany on such a move as a price for its cooperation in defense of the declining dollar.[19]

The decline of U.S. influence in the world is not solely the result of a weakened U.S. economic performance. The rapid increase over the past decade or so in Soviet military, naval, and strategic capabilities was independent of the U.S. economic decline. The latter, however, coming as it did at the time the Soviet Union was achieving strategic parity and extending its ability to intervene around the world, caused American global influence to diminish at an accelerated pace.

In brief, the national security of the United States is highly dependent on the vigor of its export performance and therefore on the strength and innovativeness of its economy. A strong domestic economy, however, is necessary but not sufficient for U.S. national security, it must also be an export-oriented economy, perceived as competing so successfully in world markets that the world demand for U.S. goods and services provides the foundation for a strong (but not necessarily appreciating) dollar. It follows that the reestablishment of U.S. power, prestige, and influence in the world requires U.S. policies that support an export-oriented economic rehabilitation.

Because of the importance of the economic and national-security implications of U.S. export policy, the current ambivalence of U.S. executive-branch proposals in the export field is troublesome. The commitment of the Reagan administration to a reestablishment of U.S. domestic economic strength is obvious and worthy of applause, but it is only part of the necessary policy package. A reinvigorated domestic economy operating at capacity with stable prices but inwardly oriented (for example, by protecting mature, relatively high-cost industries from foreign competition) would fail to reverse the decline in U.S. power and prestige worldwide. Worse, such an inward orientation would put a drag on U.S. productivity by misdirecting investment to industries where output is not as large or as highly valued as it could be.

There is, moreover, a danger that economic policies to reinvigorate the U.S. economy that are not directly inward oriented might in the context of the 1980s world economy inadvertently have the same effects. As other industrial countries undertake to reinvigorate their own economic performance by subsidizing the establishment or expansion of industries whose growth in the United States has been proven, their actions will cause a contraction of U.S. exports or a slower growth of U.S. exports if not counteracted by U.S. policy. The consequence would be a retardation in the flow of U.S. resources to growth sectors, a diversion of resources to the more-mature domestic sectors, and thus a drag on the recovery of U.S. productivity. Thus national-security arguments reinforce the economic argument in favor of a second-best policy option that involves government support for U.S. exports of commodities in whose production the United States has a clear comparative advantage.

A corollary of both the economic and national-security arguments in favor of government support for exports lies in the specific case of U.S. exports of capital goods to the developing world. During the 1970s the most rapidly growing markets in the world were to be found among the LDCs. The newly industrializing countries especially proved to have voracious appetites for machinery, construction materials and services, and the capital goods necessary for growth. The developing world now takes nearly 40 percent of U.S. exports of manufactured goods, more than the EEC and Japan combined. The LDCs take two-thirds of all U.S. motor-vehicle exports (excluding those to Canada) and about half of all U.S. machinery exports. The surging growth in these economies makes them an arena of intense competition for the industrial countries' exporters.

Despite their increasing importance in the total of U.S. exports of manufactured goods, U.S. exports to the LDCs have been slipping in relative importance. In 1970 the U.S. share of manufactured exports of Organization for Economic Cooperation and Development (OECD) countries to the LDCs was 27 percent; in 1978 it was 22 percent.[20] Although the decline in market share was not consistent and may have recovered somewhat since 1978, the trend is unequivocally down. Scholars who have studied U.S. competitiveness in Third World markets ascribe part of the reasons for the persistent decline in the U.S. share to "the fact that U.S. government taxation, export credits, and other policies and programs relating to exports are less favorable than those found in competing countries."[21]

Not only is the developing world of economic importance to the United States as a market and an important and unique source of materials in whose consumption we are not self-sufficient (many of which are crucial to our growth industries), it is of strategic importance too. The Third World is the arena where superpower confrontation is increasingly occurring. In contrast to the early postwar years when Soviet competition with the United States was concentrated on the traditional NATO-Europe target, this competition has more recently shifted to the Middle East and other Third World subregions. At the same time, Soviet policies have become increasingly assertive and adventurous in these parts of the world that are still struggling with the ongoing challenges of successful nation building. Political instability, frequently a cause or a manifestation of failed nation building, offers the Soviet Union apparently irresistable opportunities for meddling. Political instability, moreover, frequently is associated with lagging or negative economic growth. Although economic development is not sufficient to guarantee political stability, in the long run it probably is essential.

U.S. national-security interests in both the economic and political realm thus make sustained economic growth in the LDCs a matter of U.S. national concern.[22] Successful competition of U.S. exports in LDC markets will yield rewards in augmented U.S. prestige and thus of enhanced U.S. political influence. In addition, subsidized exports to these markets will permit developing countries to maintain imports of capital goods and development programs while they are adjusting to rising oil and debt-service bills.

Not all parts of the developing world are of the same degree of national-security concern to the United States. The Middle East is of immense national security interest today. One of the hazards policymakers constantly confront, however, is the inability to foresee which of those subareas of only marginal national-security concern today will rise to the top of the list tomorrow. The number of observers in 1970 who foresaw the importance to the United States of Nigeria in 1980 was scant; the same was almost as true of Saudi Arabia.

The process of development implies rising incomes and levels of consumption in the developing countries and thus expanded markets for the exports of the older industrialized countries. It also implies increasing capacities to export; indeed self-sustaining development requires an expanding ability to finance imports through exports and is thus highly dependent on the maintenance of an open world economy and growing level of world trade.

The level of indebtedness that the most rapidly growing countries have accumulated since the first oil-price shock has made them especially sensitive to interest-rate fluctuations. In some cases interest payments on outstanding indebtedness absorb one-half or more of current export earnings, leaving them little leeway for the maintenance of necessary oil and capital-goods imports. Meeting indebtedness as it falls due requires growth, which is being threatened by inability to maintain imports. This Catch-22 situation can be resolved in the short run by imports on concessionary terms. In the long run their continued economic viability will require more support from public as opposed to private sources of finance to tide them over a transition period of strain and possible default.

U.S. economic health will benefit from a sustained expansion of both exports and imports with the developing countries provided the U.S. economy remains technologically vibrant, producing a stream of new goods and services that serve a world market, and provided the economy remains flexible and capable of sustaining a shift of resources from older industries of lower productivity to the new growth industries. Such a shift is much less disruptive in an environment of expanding markets and rising incomes.

Thus U.S. national-security interest as well as U.S. economic interests argue for government support for U.S. high-technology and capital-goods exports to the developing countries. U.S. national-security interests, moreover, argue for such support in both the short and long term and quite apart from whether foreign governments continue to subsidize their exports to these markets.

2

Alternative Forms of Government Support for Exports

Chapter 1 argued that the United States in the 1980s cannot afford to ignore the importance of exports. For reasons of economic efficiency and national security, the composition, as well as the volume of exports, must be considered a high national priority. Our national-policy goal of revitalizing the economy will be successful only if the revitalization is an export-oriented effort. Such an orientation would encourage a shift of resources into the production of those goods and services where U.S. productivity is highest because these are the industries in which the United States is most efficient. Such an orientation implies a long-run shift of resources away from those industries where U.S. productivity and efficiency are lower. Thus, through an upgrading of the national-productivity average, a soundly based revitalization would result.

Given the fact that U.S. competitors in world markets employ a wide variety of subsidies to support production and export of goods and services in competition with established U.S. export industries, U.S. national interests require countermeasures. The United States must neutralize the distorting effects on its industrial structure that would otherwise be the consequence of foreign-government interference with the market mechanism. A decision by the United States to do nothing in the face of such foreign subsidies is in fact a decision to force a reallocation of U.S. resources into industries of less than maximum productivity. Such a decision will be followed by slower growth, lower real incomes, and fewer resources devoted to R&D than need be. Although there is no guaranteed one-to-one correlation between the quantity of R&D effort and productive results, the almost-certain outcome would be a slower pace of U.S. technology advance and, consequently, a further slippage of the relative strength of the United States in world markets and in the arena of world power.

Such third-best consequences can be avoided by proper public policy. Chapter 1 stressed the fact that the best public policy is one that seeks to eliminate government subsidies to exports throughout the world. While pursuing such a goal, however, prudence also requires contingency planning. The entire span of world-trade history post–World War II testifies to the ingenuity of U.S. competitors at finding new ways to pursue a mercantilist policy of protecting domestic markets while expanding foreign markets and at the same time observing the letter, if not the intent, of international agreements relating to proper trade conduct. The multiplication abroad of nontariff barriers to trade that accompanied the GATT-sponsored gradual reductions in tariff barriers through the 1960s and 1970s is the most obvious example. It would be foolish to believe that if U.S. efforts to eliminate the currently most pernicious form of export subsidies—subsidies to export finance—are successful, they will not be succeeded sooner or later by some other equally effective form of public push to exports.

Competition among U.S., European, and Japanese industries is increasingly competition among equals and thus more intense than was the case a decade or two ago. The fact that such competition is increasingly balanced is due in no small part to foreign subsidies to replicate abroad proven U.S. growth industries, and thus to change the world pattern of national comparative advantage.[1] The dirigist French or the export-driven Japanese can be counted on to devise new techniques for achieving the same ends of export support. Britain, the Low Countries, Germany, and others will not be far behind. In addition, the U.N. Conference on Trade and Development (UNCTAD) has recommended the creation of a new Export Credit Guarantee Facility to facilitate the financing of exports of manufactures from Third World countries.[2] Should such a facility come into being, even under the best of circumstances, it would add to competition for world markets by removing an existing financing disadvantage to Third World exports.

Such foreign-government support for exports will be the more intense, the slower the world economic growth. During periods of rapidly expanding world markets, such support will appear to the United States to be less onerous and thus easier to ignore, but it will be nonetheless deleterious in its sapping effects on the U.S. economy and national security. Prudence today and tomorrow requires continuous effort to remove governmental interference in world trade and to be prepared to neutralize newly emerging foreign programs that would otherwise distort U.S. resource allocation away from that which is most efficient.

GATT, of course, frowns on export subsidies, and the United States has among all the contracting parties probably been most staunch and steadfast in its support. How can support for GATT be reconciled with an unprecedented U.S. initiative that would appear to flaunt GATT rules? In fact, it seems unlikely that any formal reconciliation would be required of the United States because a U.S. program of countersubsidies would be constructed to respond to already-existing foreign-export subsidies that exist in contravention of at least the spirit of GATT. The preferred position would be one wherein every country, including the United States, obeys the spirit as well as the letter of GATT agreements. Where other contracting parties persist in flaunting both, the United States must take steps to protect its own national interests. A U.S. program of countersubsidies might aid the miscreants in seeing the error of their ways.

Government support for exports can assume a variety of forms that is almost infinite in number. Here we address only two general types of government support: subsidies for export finance and subsidies for R&D.[3] The reasons for these choices lie in the virulence of the current spate of export finance subsidies and the importance of high-technology products and services in the U.S. industrial and export structures. If one were to list U.S. industries in descending order of their comparative advantage in the United States, the list would be topped by the industries producing technologically advanced goods and services. Further down the list, the industries of lesser comparative advantage are those that would suffer a contraction of export markets should the dollar exchange rate rise by, say, 15 percent. These are industries of lesser efficiency and consequently not candidates for government support.

Government support for export finance and government support for R&D are discussed separately. On what basis should policymakers choose between the two? First, contingency planning is never a matter of "either, or" but rather a case of "both, and." It is important that the United States have available a structure of export supports that is flexible enough to neutralize foreign subsidies both when they are heavy and when they are light. It is also important that at least some of the subsidies contract as those of U.S. competitors ebb and expand as the subsidies of U.S. competitors flow, if not automatically at least with alacrity.

Research and Development

Subsidies for basic R&D designed to expand fundamental knowledge can be—indeed are—justified as in the national and world interest because they are a means of improving well-being. (Public education, especially at the higher levels, is an indirect subsidy to R&D as well as to all of industry, to say nothing of the fact that education enriches the entire life of the trainee and thus society.) Subsidies for medical research and other social objectives, which are justifiable quite apart from what U.S. competitors do, can also function as a kind of safety net to counter low-level foreign subsidies to competing industries abroad. They provide a minimum, ongoing base of support for U.S. export industries, and as long as they are about equal to the subsidies (in whatever form) given to the same industries by other governments, they would be all that is required in government support.

An example lies in U.S. government support for defense and space research. It is undertaken in the national interest, entails a significant tax burden for all elements of U.S. society, and is of direct economic benefit to only a limited number of industries and employees. (Here we are ignoring the indirect economic benefits of military security, which are immeasurable but immense.) As its results are adapted to civilian uses, however, as has frequently been the case in the past, its potential economic benefits to all of society can become enormous.[4] The same amount of research funding devoted to civilian commercial purposes would probably be more productive in economic benefits; however, the fact that such a subsidy exists (albeit unmeasured if not immeasurable) provides a margin of support for U.S. high-technology industries that would offset moderately subsidized foreign exports.

That margin, however, would diminish in scope as industry itself financed a continued stream of civilian adaptations from what was originally a defense-oriented technological advance. After some period of years the taxes paid by the growth industry on its net income, which increasingly came from adaptations that were self-financed, could repay the original government subsidy, and the remainder would be net gain to the federal government.[5] J. Fred Bucy, for example, has pointed out that early advances in the electronics industry were mostly the result of defense R&D efforts that were in turn adapted for civilian application.[6] Today the pattern is the reverse. Civilian applications have advanced so far they have considerably surpassed the military, and civilian technologies such as large-scale integrated circuitry are being employed in new weapons systems.

Export Finance

There is a limit to the amount of foreign subsidized competition that a firm in the private sector can absorb in the form of lower profits. In those intervals when foreign subsidies increase, as they are likely to do off and on, additional U.S. government support aimed at neutralizing their seriously distorting effects should be available.

The injurious economic effects on the U.S. domestic economy of heavily subsidized foreign-export credits, for example, are far more serious when market rates of interest are high. When market rates are below 8 to 10 percent, the relative importance of the interest charge in the total price of even big-ticket items is less likely to be the determining factor in which a company gets the export order. In addition, where they have greater cost efficiency, the ability of U.S. exporters to absorb some of an interest differential due to foreign subsidies is relatively greater. Thus subsidies in the form of export credits are likely to be a less-severe threat to the U.S. economy when the market rates of interest are low.

Similarly foreign-credit subsidies are more injurious to the U.S. economy when the foreign-exchange value of the dollar is relatively high. An expensive dollar makes foreign substitutes for U.S. exports more attractive in price and, in causing a contraction of U.S. exports, limits the financial resources available to U.S. exporters for meeting foreign competition.

The outlook for the level of foreign-exchange rates and market interest rates in the future depends on how successful the United States is in reducing the rate of inflation. Control over inflation in the United States, however, is not solely a function of U.S. domestic policies; even the most successful combination of U.S. fiscal and monetary policies could be frustrated by developments abroad (for example, another oil-price rise), which might once again wrench prices and therefore push interest rates sharply upward. Although corporations can sustain short-term losses from their own resources for a limited period of time, the term of the loss can never be known in advance, and there is a limit to the amount of short-term losses any private business can endure. Thus in the case of subsidized export credits, as well as other forms of export subsidies, prudence requires contingency planning and the availability of a mechanism capable of neutralizing heavy export-credit subsidies when they appear.

Such support may take a wholly different form from that of the foreign subsidy. It is not necessary to neutralize foreign subsidies that take the form of export finance by U.S. subsidies to export finance. Such a replication of the foreign-subsidy form would have the desired neutralizing effect (assuming, of course, it is of appropriate size) and thus would yield the productivity benefits that are the consequence of a countering of the foreign subsidy. In addition, it may be technically easier to fashion a temporary neutralizing subsidy on the model of the foreign offenders and thus avoid the risk that the U.S. countersubsidy will be too large or too small.

On the other hand, what is important is the bottom line. A countersubsidy can be perceived by the private sector as either an increase in revenue or a decrease in cost of sufficient size to make a competitive export contract profitable. An interest-rate subsidy on an export credit means that the exporter (or its bank) receives from the government the difference between the market rate and the lower rate at which it lends; the difference between the private sector's total revenue and total cost on the transaction is augmented by the subsidy.

It is always desirable where possible to accomplish two purposes with one strategy. If another form of countersubsidy accomplishes all of the benefits of the one modeled on the foreign form and in addition yields further cost or productivity benefits, it would be preferable. Specialized subsidies for additional R&D efforts by exporters, for example, would show up on the bottom line. All of the virtues of offsetting the effects of the foreign subsidy would be accomplished and would, in addition, have at least the potential of further augmenting productivity by raising the quality of the product or, by so changing its nature, perhaps resulting in a totally new product, further enhance sales and thus revenue.

The prospect of such a continuum through time could well give foreign governments pause in contemplating a renewal of subsidy warfare. If in fact it instead induced foreign governments to subsidize further their own R&D efforts (rather than some other form of subsidy to exports), the results could stimulate world economic growth through a deepening of the stream of new products or techniques flowing to final consumers. International competition in effective R&D can have significant beneficial effects.

Thus government support for R&D can be viewed as a complement to government support for export finance in a flexible program of export subsidies that would rise or fall as competition requires. Because the governments of most competitors of the United States in world markets increasingly have subsidized R&D in their own countries in recent years, a higher level of U.S. support for R&D can be justified on its own merits, quite apart from considerations of foreign export-finance subsidies. As a mature industrial economy, the U.S. comparative advantage will continue to lie with technologically advanced products and services only as long as this country retains a technological lead in a number of significant industries. A higher sustained level of U.S. subsidies to R&D, that is, would be in the national interest, although all that is necessary in the present context is a sporadic increase in the level of R&D subsidies.

The higher the government support for R&D, the greater the public concern with its effectiveness. A technological innovation is effective only if it is developed. In the past the research efforts of many companies have produced technology that for a variety of reasons the particular company saw fit not to develop. That this eventuality has become increasingly widespread is indicated indirectly by the growing number of technology middlemen who bring together potential buyers and sellers of technology for a fee, usually based on the royalty or lump-sum payment involved in the sale (including lease in the concept of "sale").[7] The higher the level of R&D subsidy, the more important will the function of such middlemen become in making effective the R&D subsidy. Also of increasing importance will be other mechanisms for an accelerated diffusion of knowledge about new technology and the continued growth of lively venture-capital market to provide the funds necessary to the development of new technology.

The argument thus implies that the United States could rely on R&D subsidies and an Eximbank mandated to meet foreign competition as the primary neutralizing instruments in its box of countersubsidy tools. Such a program has several advantages. It would provide increased or lowered subsidies to export finance (or still other forms of export subsidies, including additional subsidies to R&D) as the competitive situation might require. It would draw on existing institutions that currently provide support for export finance and R&D because such support is deemed to be in the national interest. The Eximbank, for example, was originally established to provide export finance in order to "supplement and encourage, and not compete with, private capital." In addition, support for R&D that is general—that is, support for basic research and the diffusion of knowledge—permits the market mechanism to determine which innovations are most effective and thus avoids any attempt to plan the course of technological advantage. As chapter 1 indicated, an attempt by the United States to plan which are to be its future growth industries would, except in conditions of extreme national emergency, be an exceptionally hazardous policy. In addition, support for defense R&D specifically directs a part of the research effort to an area of priority national interest that, judging on the basis of past performance, will also yield civilian adaptations that are directed by the market. Supplementing such support as necessary by export finance subsidies permits flexibility to adjust to varying requirements. Because the needs of U.S. exporters are so varied, however, new techniques, instruments, or institutions of providing government support for both R&D and export finance should be explored to buttress the total flexibility of the program.

3

Government Support for Exports: Research and Development

The Foreign Challenge to U.S. Preeminence in Technology

For decades U.S. superiority in technology was unquestioned. No longer is that the case. President Reagan's science adviser told an R&D conference in June 1981 that the United States has lost "preeminence in some scientific fields, while others are strongly threatened through efforts in Europe, Japan, or the Soviet Union."[1] A 1980 report of the OECD concluded that "several OECD countries narrowed—and in some sectors reversed—the lead in industrial technology taken by the United States."[2] In May 1981 the secretary of commerce warned Congress about foreign economies that are "taking dead aim on U.S. technological leadership."[3]

What is happening in the world's marketplace bears out these observations. U.S. companies are facing aggressive competition in markets they easily dominated a few years ago. Once-invincible giants like IBM and Boeing are being aggressively challenged at the technological heart of their product lines. European and Japanese high-technology companies are looking beyond invasion of U.S. markets to production within the United States. This assault on U.S. technological leadership could seriously weaken the foundations of U.S. national security. We may be witnessing a deterioration of U.S. R&D and a basic and enduring change in the American relative power position.

Because of the fundamental importance of U.S. R&D and its role in U.S. export competitiveness, these questions have been examined from many different perspectives. Several thoughtful explanations have been given. Management fundamentalists say that business leadership is infected by a new management orthodoxy that has led the nation's corporations toward short-term results and away from a commitment to compete on technological grounds.[4] Supply-side revisionists say that excessive federal intervention and inflation are bottling up commercial applications of basic science, and federal policies are steering R&D into commercial wastelands.[5] Antirevisionists say that dwindling federal support for R&D has undermined U.S. leadership in science and technology.[6] And internationalists say that a global slowdown is taking place in technological advance, with the United States slowing down more than other nations.[7]

Each of these explanations contains both a ring of truth and testimony to declining U.S. technological strength. Collectively they raise serious doubts about the adequacy, commercial clout, and relevance of U.S. R&D.

This chapter examines these subjects in an assessment of foreign R&D strategy and its implications for U.S. leadership beginning with a statistical comparison of R&D efforts of the United States and other technologically active nations; then the international challenge to U.S. leadership is examined by analyzing the strategy and actions of principal U.S. competitors; next, a critique of U.S. R&D policy is presented. The chapter concludes with a summary of the policy questions that should be addressed if the United States is to continue its leadership role in world technology in the coming years.

Spending on National R&D

International comparisons of R&D are based on national data collections that began in the early 1970s and often differ in concept and methodology. The most authoritative estimates currently available have been made by the OECD, whose collections have been carefully prepared on the basis of internationally agreed definitions in the Frascati Manual.[8] The manual is a product of many years of collaboration and testing in both OECD and in U.N. statistical committees.[9]

Despite the professional and objective intentions of OECD, the current collections of data have not yet achieved those high standards; national collections do not always follow wholly comparable definitions between countries, although definitions are consistently followed within a country through time. In addition, estimates of expenditures do not fully allow for cost differences among countries.

The comparative data for 1977, the latest year of the collection, are summarized in table 3–1.[10] These estimates show that the United States substantially overspent other major industrialized nations individually and in aggregate. They show that about 50 percent of OECD expenditures were made in the United States, and about 52 percent of industrial R&D was performed by U.S. firms. A breakdown by source of funds gives a slightly different result; industrially funded R&D in the United States was 47 percent of industrially funded R&D in the OECD countries.[11]

Data for more-recent periods would show substantially higher expenditures in current dollars but probably little change in constant dollars. Fragmentary information indicates that outlays reached a plateau in the mid-1970s and are now increasing at, or about, the rate of inflation. It is possible that the United States's expenditures in 1981 were marginally lower, relative to others, for the long-run trend prior to 1977 had been in

Table 3-1

R&D Expenditures in Principal Industrialized Nations, 1977

(billions of current U.S. dollars)

	Industrial[b]	Public[c]	Total[d]
Major industrialized nations[a]	56.02	33.28	89.30
United States	29.93	14.87	44.80
Other industrialized nations	26.09	18.41	44.50

Source: OECD, *Science Resources Newsletter No. 5* (Summer 1980).

Note: Expenditures of industrialized nations are converted to U.S. dollars at the average exchange rates for 1977.

[a]Nations included in the estimate are Australia, Belgium, Canada, Denmark, Finland, France, Germany, Iceland, Ireland, Italy, Japan, Netherlands, Norway, Sweden, Switzerland, and the United States. The United Kingdom did not submit data for this collection of 1977 R&D. We estimate U.K. R&D at about $8 billion for 1977, with industrial R&D about $5 billion, but have not included these estimates in this table.

[b]The figures given are for industrially *performed* R&D, including projects that were carried out by private companies receiving subsidies or under contract to public agencies. Figures on industrially *funded* R&D would be lower, public-funded R&D would be higher, but total expenditures would remain the same (that is, in 1977, industrially funded R&D of major industrialized nations was $42.0 billion; United States was $19.7 billion; and other industrialized nations was $22.3 billion).

[c]The figures given include R&D performed by nonprofit and higher-education institutes.

[d]Because numbers have been rounded, totals may not equal the sum of components.

that direction. As table 3-2 shows, United States R&D expenditures as a percentage of gross domestic product (GDP) were falling in the 1963-1975 period, while those of most of the other OECD members were rising.

Despite the downward trend in relative R&D expenditures, the United States performs the predominant share of international R&D and covers a wider range of humanitarian and security needs than do other nations. One consequence is the high level of exports of advanced-technology products and services. In several frontier technologies, such as data networking, satellite business communications, oil exploration and equipment, wide-bodied passenger aircraft, and software for information processing, U.S. market shares between 1975 and 1980 frequently were as high as 70 to 80 percent. Although market shares have fallen, exports in four high-technology fields—aircraft, telecommunications equipment, microprocessors, and data-processing equipment—amounted to $31 billion of the total $144 billion for all manufactured exports in 1980.[12] Technological services, royalties, licensing fees, and other invisible earnings in these fields probably added another $10 billion to $15 billion for the year. Foreign military sales,

Table 3-2
Trends of Expenditures on R&D of OECD Countries, 1963-1975
(R&D as a percentage of GDP)

	1963 (%)	1975 (%)	Index (1963 = 100)
Canada	1.00	1.00	100
France	1.60	1.80	113
Germany	1.40	2.10	150
Italy	0.60	0.90	150
Japan	1.30	1.70	131
Sweden	1.30	1.80	138
United Kingdom	2.30	2.10	91
United States	2.90	2.30	79

Source: OECD, *Technical Change and Economic Policy* (Paris: OECD, 1980).

which have a high content of advanced technology, amounted to about $15 billion.

Goods and services imports in these high-technology areas in 1980 were probably about $20 billion; U.S. net foreign-exchange earnings from high-technology goods and services probably amounted to no less than $20 billion, even excluding those in military sales.[13] U.S. net earnings surplus in high technology is still rising. The implications of the technological challenge have not yet been fully felt in international trade even though imports of several high-technology products, such as electronics equipment, small and medium-size computers, microprocessor chips, and probably software services, are rising at a more rapid rate than earnings.[14] It is perhaps only a matter of time before the net earnings in high-technology trade begin to narrow.

Foreshadowing possible future developments in the U.S. balance of payments in high-technology goods and services is the rapidly expanding effort by Japan to bolster its own R&D effort. Since about 1965 Japanese receipts from licensing its technology abroad have increased twenty-fold while its net payment position has declined (table 3-3). Japan has recently become the most important foreign source of new patents issued by the U.S. patent office; in 1975 the number of U.S. patents granted to Japan for the first time exceeded Japanese patents granted to U.S. residents (table 3-4).

Although data on current trade do not yet show a deterioration of the U.S. R&D position, examination of comparative R&D figures raises disquieting questions about the overall effectiveness of U.S. resource usage. The ratio of U.S. R&D to other OECD R&D is 1.00; that of U.S. GDP to that of other OECD GDP is 0.67.[15] These computations imply that the

Table 3–3
International Receipts and Payments of Royalties and Fees, United States and Japan, 1965–1980
(millions of U.S. dollars)

Fiscal Year	Japan			United States		
	Receipts	*Payments*	*Receipts/Payments (%)*	*Receipts*	*Payments*	*Receipts/Payments (%)*
1965	17	166	0.10	1,534	135	11.4
1966	19	192	0.10	1,515	140	10.8
1967	27	239	0.11	1,747	166	10.5
1968	34	314	0.11	1,867	186	10.0
1969	46	368	0.13	2,019	221	9.1
1970	59	433	0.14	2,331	225	10.4
1971	60	488	0.12	2,545	241	10.6
1972	74	572	0.13	2,770	294	9.4
1973	88	715	0.12	3,225	385	8.4
1974	113	718	0.16	3,821	346	11.0
1975	161	712	0.23	4,300	473	9.1
1976	173	846	0.20	4,353	482	9.0
1977	233	1,027	0.23	4,806	439	10.9
1978	274	1,241	0.22	5,760	607	9.5
1979	342	1,260	0.27	6,048	757	8.0
1980	—		—	7,135	769	9.3

Source: Research and Statistics Department, Bank of Japan, Technical Trade Table, *Economic Statistics Annual 1980* (March 1981), p. 240; U.S. Department of Commerce, Bureau of Economic Analysis, *Survey of Current Business* 61 (June 1981):38–39.

Table 3–4
U.S. Patent Balance with Japan, 1966–1975

	Granted by Japan to U.S. Residents	*Granted by United States to Japanese Residents*
1966	4,683	1,122
1969	4,657	2,152
1972	5,948	5,154
1975	4,918	6,339

Source: U.S. National Science Board, *Science Indicators* (Washington, D.C.: National Science Board, 1977).

United States funds and performs about one-half of all Western R&D but does it from only two-fifths of overall production. These or comparable data are often used to show that other countries are not carrying their weight in international R&D. This is doubtlessly true. The data also suggest that the rest of the world may be able to generate much more national production from R&D expenditures than does the United States or that others may make better and more-extensive use of innovations from R&D than does the United States.[16] A dollar spent on industrial R&D in the United States is associated with $53 of gross national product; but for Canada the association is $167; for Japan, $77; for Germany, $63; and for France, $71.[17] Because of the lag between R&D effort and its indeterminate commercial result, the difference in effectiveness (indicated by this association) could vary considerably from year to year. If, however, the international relationship of these magnitudes remains roughly constant, the difference in effectiveness would be cumulatively significant.

Without questioning the imprecision of these data as indicators of commercial effectiveness or that many other factors enter into national production, the data nonetheless raise doubts about the commercial efficiency of U.S. research and development.[18] U.S. competitors have compensated for the larger U.S. expenditures on R&D by concentrating on commercially effective R&D, by practicing replicative and adaptive technology strategies that compensate for the advantages of U.S. technological leadership, and by following systematic policies and programs of support that are targeted at specific high-technology objectives.

An International Strategy for Low Spenders

All governments provide financial support for commercial R&D and subsidize this activity in many ways, direct and indirect. There is a high correlation between government support and successful commercial accomplishment, particularly when a subsidy is targeted toward a specific commercial technology objective. For some high-cost technologies, subsidized R&D spells the difference between success and failure. In total public R&D support, however, other nations tend to spend less than the United States. How can one account for the deteriorating U.S. technological competitiveness in the face of disproportionately high expenditure levels?

A Yen Saved Is a Dollar Earned

Those who are outspent by the United States must find some way to get by on less money. One way to compensate is to avoid forms of R&D that have little direct commercial impact. Commercial success can be as much a product of what is not done as of what is done. When the most distinctive feature of present-day R&D is the high-cost project, judicious use of resources is essential and makes it possible to concentrate human and financial resources where they count most.

Basic Research: Basic research is an expensive form of national scientific investment. Any payoff is to all humanity and is not collectible nationally. In the past, an originator of scientific breakthrough enjoyed a certain lead time over others. Accelerated diffusion of knowledge has greatly compressed the duration of this advantage, however. For most nations the cost of basic research has become a simple opportunity cost, to be measured by the commercial application and development research that is foregone when basic research is carried out. Commercially it is good news when a Nobel prize is awarded to some other nation for a scientific breakthrough that is widely accessible. There may be more than symbolism in that the Nobel awards for the past thirty years in physics, engineering, and chemistry have gone to sixty-five Americans and twenty-nine British and only seven Germans and two Japanese.[19]

It is bad news for everybody, however, when basic research is neglected everywhere. Although there is universal recognition that fundamental scientific knowledge is ultimately essential for commercial innovation and development, there is also dwindling enthusiasm for allocating corporate or government resources for scientific work. Fading support is widespread. It is most consequential when it happens in the United States, the world's spawning ground for new ideas in high technology. An OECD study has concluded that downward trends in industrial basic research prevailed throughout the 1970s; there was a relative decline for most nations and an absolute decline for the United States.[20] Most nations—Japan was an exception—ended two decades of steadily rising R&D in universities as support leveled off in real terms in the 1970s.

The trend of U.S. government expenditures for basic research has contributed to the general worldwide malaise. Despite rising annual outlays, they are now lower in constant dollars than in 1965. In comparative terms, however, they continue to be larger than other nations, and with about $5.9 billion allocated for basic research (12 percent for defense) in the 1982 federal budget, the United States will probably be spending substantially more on basic research than any other OECD government.[21]

It is not that governments fail to recognize the value of basic research. According to OECD data, many allocate as much as 30 to 50 percent of government R&D expenditures for "general advancement of knowledge," but that phrase is often a euphemism that covers applied research as well as research for basic scientific knowledge.[22] The high cost of much modern basic research is the obstacle. Scientific communities everywhere tend to be active advocates of international collaboration on high-cost research, but governments, strapped for funds and fighting inflationary budgets, have other pressing priorities. In both the United States and other countries, high-cost basic research projects, such as the Glomar Explorer, solar-polar exploration, gamma-ray astronomy, synthetic fuels, and exploration of the outer planets, are vulnerable targets for budget cutting.

Social Overhead R&D: Another way for a nation to economize its R&D resources is by minimizing expenditures on social-overhead R&D. Social-overhead expenditures include R&D for health, quality of life (for example, the environment), and defense. Spending for these purposes is akin to outlays for basic research in that such spending may have an important secondary effect on commercial vitality, but it is an indirect effect and may be very remote. Indeed R&D in health, quality of life, and defense have direct objectives that justify them apart from their economic effects.

The most recent OECD data for 1977 show all other major industrial nations falling substantially below the United States in all categories of social overhead expenditures. Table 3–5 indicates, for example, that Japan's social overhead R&D amounted to only one-tenth of 1 percent of GDP. Except for Italy, Japan spent less for social overhead R&D than did any other industrialized nation. The United States, on the other hand, spent proportionately ten times as much as Japan. With social overhead R&D amounting to nearly 1 percent of GDP, U.S. expenditures were the largest by far of any other industrialized nation.

Although disparities are found in all three categories of social overhead, they are most pronounced in health. In fighting disease through science, the United States provides about 75 percent of all health R&D expenditures in the industrialized world.

What table 3–5 signifies is highly relevant to the commercial effectiveness of U.S. R&D. Other nations may spend significantly less than the

Table 3-5
Resources for Social-Overhead R&D, 1977

Country	Quality of Life	Health	Defense	Total
Canada[a]	9.4	5.4	3.4	18.2
France	10.8	4.9	30.6	46.3
Germany	11.5	3.9	13.4	28.8
Italy	2.7	1.4	1.9	6.0
Japan[b]	5.9	2.9	1.1	9.9
United Kingdom	6.1	2.3	57.6	66.0
United States	15.0	14.0	65.8	94.8

Source: OECD, *Technical Change and Economic Policy* (Paris: OECD, 1980).
Note: Figures are 1/100 percent of GDP.
[a]Data are for 1976.
[b]Data are for 1975.

United States on overall R&D. By economizing on social overhead they are able to channel significantly more money into commercially beneficial uses. The United States, conversely, puts proportionately more into social overhead, and expenditures for commerically beneficial R&D are proportionately smaller. This is not to deny that social-overhead R&D can have significant commercially effective adaptations, but the time lags here are likely to be long and have little bearing on technological competition. In addition, some observers have suggested that civilian adaptations of military R&D, such as those that have been commercially important in the past, are becoming more remote and therefore less likely in the future.[23]

The effect of these differing patterns of allocation is most significant for Germany and Japan, the principal technological competitors of the United States. The estimates presented in table 3-6 show how German and Japanese spending on basic research and social-overhead R&D affect comparison of their commercial R&D with that of the United States.

These estimates show a much narrower gap in commercially effective R&D when disparities in overhead R&D and basic research are taken into account. Although Germany and Japan in 1977 spent only 25 and 32 percent as much as the United States in total R&D, their commercially effective R&D was closer to the United States—30 and 49 percent, respectively.

When commercially effective R&D is estimated by subtracting from total R&D the expenditures on social overhead and basic research, it becomes evident that Germany and Japan have a much greater concentration of R&D where it is commercially valuable. By minimizing the use of resources where commercial returns are remote, indirect, or marginal,

Table 3-6
Commercially Effective R&D: Germany, Japan, and the United States, 1977
(millions of U.S. dollars)

	Total R&D		Commercially Effective R&D		Coefficient Commercial Effectiveness
	Amount	Percent of GDP[a]	Amount	Percent of GDP[a]	
Germany	11,083	210	6,184	117	56
Japan	14,234	190	10,035	134	71
United States	44,800	240	20,608	110	46
France	6,754	180	4,053	108	69
United Kingdom[c]	8,000[b]	210	4,800[b]	120	52

Source: OECD, *Science Resources Newsletter No. 5* (Summer 1980); OECD, *Technical Change and Economic Policy* (Paris: OECD, 1980).

[a]One one-hundredth of 1 percent.

[b]Our estimate from other OECD sources; not completely comparable with other data.

[c]1975.

Japan and Germany are able to place a higher proportion of their R&D where its impact on output and exportables is immediate. More than 71 percent of Japan's R&D is targeted for commercially effective purposes, whereas the equivalent in Germany is about 56 percent and 46 percent for the United States.

Second-Strike Technology

Avoiding commercially unrewarding spending is one way that other nations compensate for the much larger R&D expenditures of the United States. Other measures also help. A favored approach, to replicate successful innovations developed elsewhere, is second-strike technology. Of the more than fifty venture firms in biotechnology and genetic engineering, almost all are in the United States and all but one of the top seven is American.[24] This has become a familiar pattern in the past forty years, with Americans habitually being the first entrants into new technology areas. How deeply ingrained the second-strike habit has become is shown in Prime Minister Margaret Thatcher's proposal to the Automan 1981 conference on automation when she said, "We must make sure that even if Britain is not in the forefront in the first generation of robotics, we are well up when it comes to the second."[25]

There are obvious advantages in a first-strike strategy, and it has dominated much of American thinking about technology innovation. Yet a second-strike strategy can compensate for many of the first-strike advantages. The second strike is less expensive. The United States spent $2.4 billion in developing the large integrated-circuit technology, which Germany and Japan were able to replicate later for about $500 million each.[26] Commercially, second-strike technology can be more rewarding, both for the entrepreneur and for the entrepreneur's society. Many companies have found that research collection of what others have done is more rewarding than original work, and they allocate R&D funds accordingly. The European Industrial Research Managers Association concluded that the most successful innovators are not the first strikers but the companies whose R&D efforts are thoroughly integrated with the rest of their business.[27] The successful innovator concentrates more on production efficiency and less on product pathbreaking. An important advantage of second-strike technology is its easier adaptability to long production runs and mass assembly. Second-strike technology is suitable for an established firm that is able to concentrate its engineering skills on market competition where cost margins are as important as innovative approaches. Second strikers have survival qualities for the long run when the payoff is maximized for a nation's job and income levels.

A prerequisite for the second-strike technology is access to the first-striker's experience. Like Thatcher's automation entrepreneurs, Japanese and German medical firms are already preparing for the second generation of commercialized development of genetic engineering. Japanese firms are negotiating to buy American advanced genetic-engineering techniques because, says the managing director of Japan's Green Cross, "it is too late for the fundamental work."[28] And Germany's Hoechst company has signed a $50 million agreement with Massachusetts General Hospital to have access to both existing technology and the research resources of the institution.[29] The importance that other countries attach to replication is evidenced by the number of scientifically trained representatives they post in the United States. France, for example, has nine science attaches in the United States whose job is to follow R&D at both the national and the laboratory level.[30]

Japan's development of very large scale integrated (VLSI) circuit technology is a recent second-strike success story. The semiconductor industry originated in the United States in the early 1950s. It rapidly spread to other countries, particularly to Japan, where semiconductor production provided the base for the products of many of the world's leading consumer-electronic companies. By 1976 the U.S. semiconductor industry had taken on a new coloration. With a $2.4 billion R&D program funded jointly by private and government sources, the VSLI circuitry was mastered, and a major new world industry had evolved, dominated by U.S. firms.[31]

Japan's semiconductor production at that time was about 40 percent that of the United States, made up primarily of discrete components for consumer electronic products. The growing industrial demand for integrated circuits convinced the Ministry of International Trade and Industry (MITI) of the need for stimulating Japanese capabilities for integrated-circuit production. MITI organized the VLSI Technology Research Association in 1976, consisting of the five largest electronic firms, for catching up on U.S. production technology of the 16,000- and 64,000-bit microchip and overtaking the U.S. technological lead on the 256,000-bit integrated circuit.[32]

MITI's contribution to the VLSI program was modest, paying one-third of the half-billion dollar cost and persuading corporate competitors to collaborate. There is no question of the success of the program. It enabled Japanese firms to catch up with the United States and greatly reduced the production cost of microchips. The VLSI project came up with production processes that reduced defects in chips and quality control that raised Japanese yields of usable chips far above American yields.[33] In 1980 Japanese firms marketed 40 percent of the 16,000-bit devices and 60 percent of the 64,000-bit devices sold in the world market. Japan's exports of integrated circuits exceeded by a wide margin those of the United States.

The program's most important consequence was to give Japanese industry access to microchips needed for computerizing production processes at home. The Japanese Management Association considers the microchip as having value not in itself or in a stand-alone computer but when "attached to various machines or household appliances where the special uses and applications create products with a very high added value."[34] More than 70 percent of the world's robots, for example, are working today on Japanese production lines.[35] Many have been imported from the United States, but domestic robot production is growing at 40 to 50 percent a year.[36] This rapid assimilation of integrated circuits into production and assembly of virtually all machine-using industries has been a major factor in the growing Japanese lead in industrial productivity.

Technology by Osmosis

In an age of high-cost science and technology, alert technology strategists must find ways to gain entry into new high-technology industries. One way is to buy access to basic knowledge, as some companies are now doing for genetic-engineering technology. Another is to engage a special R&D project, like MITI's integrated-circuit effort. A third is technology by osmosis, which requires patience and persistence.

Technology osmosis is a natural outgrowth of widespread acceptance of principles of free diffusion of scientific and technological knowledge and of the relatively open investment and contracting procedures that have become the practice in most international industries. An articulate advocate of the corporate policies that abet technology by osmosis is Michael Blumenthal, chairman of the Burroughs Corporation. In a recent speech, Blumenthal said, "Our dealings abroad, then, must be cooperative ones, creating partnerships with companies in developed countries and establishing technology transfers in the Third World. Cooperative ventures help to break down the walls of mistrust between nations and to reestablish the marketplace as the arbiter of a product's worth."[37]

Most corporate executives and indeed most thoughtful citizens would probably agree with Blumenthal's view that widespread diffusion of knowledge is desirable. The practical consequences may be traced in the evolution of satellite communications and wide-bodied, passenger aircraft.

Satellite Communications: For nearly two decades satellite communications have been dominated by the United States, the result of launch and miniaturized communication technologies acquired through U.S. defense and space R&D. When the International Telecommunications Satellite Organization (INTELSAT) was established in 1964, the United States was the initiator, the sole source of the technology, and, with 28 percent of the shares, the principal financing participant.[38]

Today the original 11 shareholders have grown to 104 nations; INTELSAT handles two-thirds of all transoceanic communications and a large part of internal communications for many countries. It has all but eliminated distance as a cost factor in international communications. Although the initial INTELSAT technology came from the United States, the production process today is much more diffused. In 1964 only the Soviet Union and the United States were capable of placing a satellite in orbit. Five more nations—France, China, India, the United Kingdom, and Japan—now have that capability, and Brazil will soon have it.

Many national and international organizations have capabilities in the production of satellites that are used for communications and for other purposes, such as weather observation, resource mapping, and ocean shipping. Japan, Canada, Indonesia, India, France, and Germany have their own satellites in orbit, in most cases launched by the National Aeronautics and Space Administration (NASA). In almost all instances, development of these national satellites has leaned heavily on U.S. technologies. The most advanced broadcast satellite in use today, for example, is a Japanese satellite made by General Electric in New Jersey. All of the Canadian satellites have been manufactured under U.S. prime contractors.

A significant change has taken place in the production of a communication satellite since INTELSAT I was launched in 1965. INTELSAT V is the fifth generation in the line. Ford Aerospace and Communication Corporation (FACC) in Palo Alto, California, is the prime contractor for INTELSAT V, with orders and options for fifteen such satellites to be launched in 1981 and later. A large part of the production is subcontracted by FACC outside the United States. GEC-Marconi of the United Kingdom is supplying the beacon transmitters; Messerschmitt Bolkow Blohm of Germany, the attitude control and sun-tracking array; Mitsubishi of Japan, the earth-coverage aerials; and CSF-Thomson and Aerospatiale of France the radio-frequency power generators, the body structures, and the thermal-control systems.[39] As the prime contractor, FACC has the critical tasks of designing the package, integrating its production, and testing the completed structure and all of its working and control components.

Because of the high R&D costs of satellite communications and the rapid pace of development of a technologically active industry, it has taken other nations several years to reach competitive status. Neither Japan nor Europe has a seasoned national FACC to turn to today; yet they have a wide spectrum of components capabilities and are capable of satellite design and construction on their own. Aerospatiale of France, with FACC, is building the Arabsat communication system for use in the Middle East.[40] France and Germany are constructing a three-channel direct broadcast satellite, which they expect to place in operation in 1983.[41] British Aerospace is the main contractor for the European Space Agency's L-SAT, which will provide broadcast channels as well as telecommunication channels in Europe and is preparing itself for building and marketing fifty to sixty satellites in the next twenty years.[42]

The European Space Agency (ESA) currently is offering some commercial launching services.[43] Recent press reports indicate that its affiliate, Arianespace, has been awarded a $50 million contract for launching two communication satellites for General Telephone and Electronics (GTE) in 1984. This is the first contract that Arianespace, formed in 1980 to finance, produce, market, and launch ESA rockets, has received from an American customer. An authoritative observer concludes that it is "just a matter of time before other nations become self-sufficient or competitive in the satellite areas."[44]

Aircraft Manufacture: The high cost of R&D for jet passenger aircraft has been a compelling constraint on the growth of competition in the industry. In the past twenty-five years the Boeing Company has resisted the collaboration that produces technology osmosis and has managed to operate its civilian-aircraft unit profitably. Some other American and European manufacturers have produced aircraft for narrow portions of the overall market. This has generally resulted in losses that have been subsidized by governments or other corporate operations. No aircraft producer has been able to develop a line that could challenge the supremacy of Boeing.

In the past decade, however, the heavily subsidized European consortium of Airbus Industrie has been established to emulate and compete with Boeing. One area of head-on competition is the development of the 150-passenger aircraft. According to the *Economist,* the nonrecurring cost for developing a new 150-passenger aircraft is estimated at about $1.5 billion (not including engines) for a single company or consortium.[45] Cost recovery, under optimistic assumptions, will take until 1997 if the first production deliveries can be made in 1986. Counting the R&D costs for engines to power the 150-passenger airplanes, total nonrecurring investment of $7.5 billion is in prospect over the next five to six years.

What is novel is not just the high cost of developing this generation airplane but the prospect of meeting these high costs in a context of head-on international competition. Rarely has a single corporation dominated a major global industry as Boeing has over the past twenty-five years. OPEC, however, has changed a fundamental factor in Boeing's family designs. In the early 1970s, when development of Boeing's present family began, fuel accounted for less than 15 percent of airline operating costs and capital depreciation for 25 percent. In 1985 fuel expense is expected to be 33 percent and capital depreciation 8 percent of operating costs.[46] With such a drastic change in operating costs, airlines are looking for fuel efficiencies far greater than Boeing or other manufacturers provided in the past and for closer balances between aircraft capacities and traffic requirements. A wholly new lineup of aircraft is necessary, giving other manufacturers a chance to cut into Boeing's predominance in the world's passenger-aircraft market.

Airbus Industrie is the competition that Boeing needs to fear most. Although still receiving substantial subsidies from its principal backers in Germany, France, and the United Kingdom, Airbus has made substantial sales of the A-300 in Europe and Japan and is second only to Boeing in current overall sales volume. By 1984 Airbus Industrie will add two new models that compete with Boeing's new 767 and the proposed 150-passenger airplane.[47] Airbus Industrie clearly is aiming at a family of its own that will compete across the board with Boeing.

Boeing's answer is to expand its family by three additional members.[48] With the 707 phased out, the company will be marketing five models ranging from the 115-passenger 737-200, to a 747 that will carry over 400 passengers. The Boeing strategy will make it difficult for competitors who go after a narrow portion of the market and will put greater pressure on Airbus to develop additional models. Boeing is raising the stakes for Airbus competition in the expectation that its supporters will back away from financing losing propositions.

Boeing's strategy may expose the company to financial pressures engendered by the high cost of R&D that will be undertaken. In addition to the expenses of developing the 757 and the 767, the company is also upgrading the 737 and 747 models. If the expected announcement is made in 1982 on the new 150-passenger aircraft, Boeing will have about $3 billion to $4 billion committed in R&D for new and redesigned aircraft. Its own financial resources will be deeply committed until returns begin rolling in from the new airplanes. A tie-up with a Japanese collaborator might provide insurance that sales will go well there and provide additional capital. Thus Boeing may opt for a technology-osmosis answer. Under pressure from the heavily subsidized Airbus, it may break with its own tradition and seek foreign collaborators (as opposed to subcontractors) who could both share financing risks and ease marketing problems abroad.

Promoting Home-Front Technology Abroad

All governments strive for a home-front environment in which domestic industry will invest in productive technologies that are internationally competitive. In recent years, many have introduced more-active programs in the belief that measures that stimulate industrial innovations will help solve pressing national or local economic problems. Between 1977 and 1980, major new innovation programs were adopted or strengthened by Austria, Belgium, Canada, Denmark, France, Germany, Japan, the Netherlands, Sweden, and the United Kingdom. In addition, an increasing number of newly industrializing countries have turned to more-complex production technologies and have begun to strengthen internal capabilities for technology production.

The Helping Hand

Direct support is the favored route for stimulating technological growth. These governments consider direct support an effective means of placing limited funds where they are needed most. They generally approach technology stimulation not as an abstract issue but as a partial answer to specific current problems. Common current problems for which technology stimulation is perceived as the answer include reviving a depressed area or a troubled industrial sector, fighting recession and solving structural maladjustments, and, in the newly industrializing countries of the Third World, financing imports of higher-priced oil while maintaining relatively rapid rates of economic development. No government views technology as the sole answer to any of these problems. Most regard technology advance as an effective tool in conjunction with other measures and consider targeted support as the approach most likely to work.

The Netherlands program, adopted in November 1979, is typical of those in other countries.[49] The program, implemented jointly by the Ministry of Economic Affairs and the Ministry for Science and Research, provides for additional funding for innovation support in a five-year commitment of about $160 million per year above normal expenditures in the R&D budget. The program calls for cooperative research institutes that are jointly financed by government and industry and that normally include an association of companies rather than a single enterprise. Companies that have unique problems may receive direct subsidies covering up to 30 percent of costs for either in-house or contract research.

In addition to direct subsidies, the Dutch program also provides for development credits for risky start-up projects. The Dutch government may lend as much as 70 percent of total costs for important projects, a sum that is repayable if the project proves to be successful. The Spearhead Fund permits the government to participate in equity financing of high-risk companies that are introducing new technologies.

Direct support in other countries differs from the Netherlands only in detail. Funding for the innovation-support programs tends to be significant though perhaps not lavish. The German program provides up to 50 percent grants (repayable if successful) for high-risk technology innovators and two-thirds for some engineering projects. France subsidizes as much as 50 to 75 percent of fundamental and applied research costs of approved firms.[50] The Mitterrand administration's policy hinges importantly on stimulating high-technology industrial growth by a real increase in research spending of 11 percent a year for four years with the goal of surpassing the United States in percentage of GNP devoted to R&D.[51] Italy's program is more generous than others, providing up to 90 percent of costs on some R&D projects, but it allocates insignificant sums for the effort.[52] With few exceptions, the technology-stimulation programs, like that of Japan, permit government equity participation in high-risk development projects.

Friendly Tax Collectors

Tax incentives are regarded by other OECD governments as less useful than direct grants or credits for energizing technological activity. Because the effect of tax incentives is indirect and corporate tax laws are complex, the connection between tax measures and technology advance is regarded as unreliable. Tax incentives are regarded as more likely to benefit flourishing companies and established firms rather than those that need help.[53]

Nevertheless several governments provide some tax benefits for R&D. Canada permits both capital and current expenditures as a deductible cost item in the year the cost is incurred. Small Canadian firms are allowed a tax credit of 25 percent of R&D operating expenses. All firms are allowed a tax credit of 50 percent of any increase above the previous three-year average R&D outlay.

European governments make less-extensive use of tax incentives than does Canada. Some, including the Netherlands and the United Kingdom, treat R&D expenditures no differently from other current or depreciable costs. France permits accelerated depreciation (two years) for expenditures on plants and buildings. Germany allows a 20 percent tax credit on a limited portion of an R&D investment. Japan allows a 20 percent tax credit on incremental R&D expenditures and permits some firms to take an accelerated depreciation on R&D capital outlays, one-sixth more than normal in the first year. An important tax factor in Japan is the credit of 25 to 35 percent allowed on earnings from technology sales abroad.

Venture Capital for New Technology

Virtually all governments have special arrangements for providing venture capital for high-risk development projects. Private venture-capital facilities tend to be thinner than in the United States. Demand for risk capital is light, however, and government-supported facilities are intended more to stimulate demand than to fill an unsatisfied market.

A variety of government programs is followed for venture-capital financing. In Germany both the federal government and the provincial governments provide loan and credit guarantees for R&D. The federal government also provides loan guarantees and financial backing for several risk-capital banks. Consequently these privately operated banks are able to lend at favorable rates of interest. They have found some receptivity for these loans, mainly from new enterprises in economically disadvantaged areas. The federal government has recently introduced a new program for topping up capital of new firms with low-interest, twenty-year loans.

The private venture-capital market in Japan is primarily confined to large firms, which provide most funding for new ventures. In addition, MITI has set up the Center for Development of R&D Oriented Enterprises, which provides guarantees for loans for innovation projects and other R&D requirements of small and medium firms that have high-technology capacity or potential. The center has about $9 million for its annual operations, plus a guarantee fund supported by both government and corporate subscribers.

Canada has an extensive government facility for venture capital. The Federal Business Development Bank offers loans, loan guarantees, leasing, or equity financing. In high-risk situations, the bank may take an equity position, which can be repurchased when the company is showing a profit. In 1978 the bank had about $1.5 billion in outstanding loans to thirty-three firms.

The United Kingdom operates an extensive support program for venture capital. The Industrial and Commercial Finance Corporation has functioned since 1945, providing loans and equity capital for high-technology start-up firms. The National Enterprise Board (NEB), established to promote industrial efficiency in international competitiveness, provides equity financing for advanced-technology ventures. The NEB expects at least 20 percent equity in its ventures and provides loan capital as well; however, it does not provide financing for either new inventions or for ventures still in prototype.

The Technology Nanny

Essentially the function of a government nanny is to help spread know-how and aid companies in applying existing advanced technology, to help companies organize themselves to adapt existing technology to their own requirements, and to organize themselves to do further technological research to improve the efficiency of their operation. Almost all countries have a special body designed to facilitate the accomplishment of these goals through a continuous public-private dialogue. Germany, Italy, and Austria rely on private associations, particularly their chambers of commerce, to fill the functions of a nanny. Recently the Netherlands and France have begun to strengthen their systems for applying technology innovation.

The United Kingdom has a highly organized system, largely installed since about 1975. The Industrial Cooperative Research Association has a subsidized budget of $20 million and provides ready access to both domestic and foreign know-how for most branches of Britain's industry. A five-year program, begun in 1978, supports the United Kingdom's microelectronics-components industry. The Product and Process Development scheme, introduced in 1977, assists companies in developing and launching new or improved products and processes, working primarily with small and medium-sized companies. The Design Council promotes improved design of British products through advisory services, publications, and informational displays.

One of Britain's successful ventures in industrial innovation is its Microprocessors Applications Project (MAP) launched in 1978. It is intended to encourage the employment of microprocessors in products and processes. With a budget of more than $100 million, the MAP program covers all aspects of the introduction of microprocessors. Workshops and seminars are held to inform industrialists and trade unions of the potential of microprocessors. Training courses are given to company officers responsible for factory operations. MAP also provides consultancy assistance to assess the potential of using microelectronic devices in a company's products or processes. Grants are available through MAP for up to 25 percent of the development cost of an application. Companies can also obtain specific counseling on the introduction of automation and robotics in their operations.

Japan's nanny is the well-known MITI. Functioning with a modest operational budget of less than $200 million, MITI relies less on money and more on its ability to come up with imaginative schemes to solve Japan's industrial problems. MITI is organized on industrial lines, with active committee systems in all principal industries. These committees serve as the channels through which know-how can be disseminated. MITI's principal interests are in the larger enterprises, and it pays special attention to promoting growth of high technology.

Less well known is the system of prefectural laboratories, an interrelated group of 195 R&D centers. They are located throughout Japan, in both large and small cities, and employ some 6,600 persons. Their primary function is technical assistance and diffusion of technological information, accomplished through document dissemination, technical seminars, and counseling on plant and factory problems. Although the prefectural program has a small budget, it provides counseling for fourteen thousand plants and factories a year.

Public Writs and Private Rights

A major determinant of technology growth is the competitive framework in which R&D is expected to produce beneficial results. Specific policy issues that bear on the competitive framework include control and regulation of concentrated industrial power, patent rights, and government contracts.

Most nations deal with monopoly power as a problem that should be answered in terms of public ownership. Antitrust legislation has been adopted by a few but tends not to be regarded as a significant tool for maintaining competitive conditions. Indeed much important industrial R&D, particularly in Japan, might be impermissible under U.S. conceptions of antitrust law. Japan's antitrust law, which dates back to 1947, permits small and medium-sized companies to collaborate in sales; in addition, targeted industries frequently have been given exemptions from antitrust provisions to permit collaboration in R&D. For example, MITI's consortium for the VLSI circuits brought together the five largest computer manufacturers in Japan. A large number of MITI's initiatives have been carried out under such arrangements.

Although MITI's R&D activities tend to be targeted to specific technological problems, many of the European cooperative efforts involve more-lasting combinations of competing companies. The industrial research associations, favored by a number of European countries, would probably be closely observed by antitrust groups in the United States. Although industrial research associations abound and frequently receive government grants in the United Kingdom, Norway, Sweden, Italy, France, Germany, and Belgium, they are rare in the United States.

Government contracting and procurement have been widely used by other countries as a means for promoting national interests. All governments carefully police contracting and procurement and generally favor domestic procedures but not necessarily new technology procedures. The new industrial-innovation programs adopted since 1977, however, have introduced a greater awareness of how government purchasing power might be used. Several nations, including Sweden, Denmark, the Netherlands, and Germany, are strengthening contract and procurement policies to favor innovative and high-technology suppliers. Japan is ahead of the others in this regard. One of MITI's functions is to draw up procurement policy goals and targets that, after cabinet approval, become the government guide.

Many governments follow aggressive policies for encouraging patents, protecting the rights of investors, and providing for widespread dissemination of inventions. Germany taxes income from inventions at half normal rates and exempts lump-sum payments altogether. France has simplified patent rules, in hope of removing an obstacle to the use of patent protection, and has also clarified patent protections for service inventions. Several countries have extensive distribution systems for patent literature. Japan's patent office provides up-to-date worldwide source materials on patents and industrial properties through a nationwide library system. The Patent Office Information Center has a computerized research system with both domestic and foreign documentation in the data base. The United Kingdom has a similar system, also available throughout the world, but, in contrast to Japan, reportedly it is little used.

Third World Technological Advance

In the past, the Third World has tended to use simpler technologies and production processes, and the commercial trade of its members has prospered more on low-cost labor than on technical skills or capital-intensive investment. More recently, the rapidly growing, newly industrializing countries (NICs)—Brazil, Mexico, Singapore, South Korea, and Taiwan, for example—have reached the stage where higher volumes of national savings, stronger capital-raising capabilities, and the formation of technological cadres support the use of more-complex technologies. A combination of rising average skill levels in their labor forces, rising real wages, and competition from lower-wage, less-developed countries has led the NICs to shift the emphasis of their development programs increasingly toward industries of more-advanced technology. Like most of the OECD countries, the NICs' efforts in R&D are almost exclusively the application of existing technology within the context of their own national programs of economic development and their current problems of structural maladjustment.

Mexico's R&D establishments, for example, are concerned primarily with infrastructure and natural-resource development, with much emphasis on petroleum and food. Mexico has serious intentions of becoming a major factor in international markets for petroleum-related products, as well as in other traditional industries such as automobiles, steel, and machinery. Brazil's overwhelming dependence on imported oil led it into biomass research aimed at developing an ethyl alcohol or methanol substitute for gasoline. This and other high-cost manufacturing—computers and telecommunications, for example—are prime candidates for subsidized high-technology exports. Singapore, Taiwan, and South Korea are using public support for high-technology specialty production, thus shifting their industrial structures increasingly toward the upper reaches of the technology spectrum.

Taken together, the advancing maturity of technology in the NICs and the more-intense R&D efforts of the other OECD countries pose a challenge to the United States. If the United States does not maintain the flow of innovation necessary to support a rising level of exports in world markets, its standard of living sooner or later will be depressed and its national security increasingly threatened.

Policy Strategy of the Main Challengers

Other nations have had to pay close attention to technology policy or fall hopelessly behind the U.S. technological lead. Japan and most governments in Europe have made strong commitments to competitive growth. The specific measures of support have been most effective when systematically employed in an R&D strategy with clear competitive objectives.

An examination of the policy and strategy approaches of three industrialized countries, Japan, Germany, and France, will show how policymaking in three different cultures can be focused on the complexities of technology policy and how the intricate technology policy relationships between the government and the private sector can be brought to bear on competitive growth.

Japan: Still Number Two

Japan's R&D expenditures are the second largest in the world, now surpassing Germany and exceeded only by the United States.[54] Buildup of the R&D structure has been impressive, with overall expenditures rising fivefold in a decade when GDP was doubling. As U.S. real R&D expenditures were falling, Japan moved significantly closer in total effort. Despite the closing gap, however, Japanese R&D expenditures are less than one-third those of the United States.

Japanese R&D expenditures come primarily from private industry. With only 30 percent of total funding from government budgets, a Japanese prime minister has limited direct finances for moving R&D in the desired direction. In 1978, for example, the director of science and technology had the largest single R&D budget in the entire government.[55] It amounted to $1.1 billion and was the financing source of programs in energy, space, marine development, remote sensing, and promotion of science and technology. MITI's budget for supporting industrial R&D in 1978 was $281 million. Eleven U.S. federal agencies had more in their budgets.

A Japanese government has other ways of directing R&D toward desired objectives. In important respects, the government plays a much more active role in industrial R&D than does the United States. MITI has a powerful influence over industrial corporations and is able to use institutional leverage effectively. Its approval of an industrial venture makes bank financing much easier. In a country where loan financing, rather than equity financing, is the normal route for expansion, MITI's backing carries great weight in industrial decisions to undertake research or to embark on innovative ventures. Targeted industries typically have enjoyed special R&D tax benefits more liberal than those in the United States. Tax credits are allowed for incremental R&D to industry generally, and generous exemptions are permitted for earnings on exports of technology. MITI's intercession with taxing authorities, especially on questions of international consequence, has often been advantageous for targeted industries. MITI, however, is a technology nanny, not a technology financier. It exercises influence through the slower, subtle processes of consensus much more than through budgetary inducements.

For many years the Japanese industrial-government complex acted on the fundamental consensus that Japan's R&D should concentrate on adapting borrowed ideas, depending heavily on U.S. technological leadership. A sense of vulnerability to dependency on outside forces has emerged in recent years. A major cabinet report and white paper prepared by the Council on Science and Technology, part of the prime minister's executive office, spelled out the dilemma that Japan was facing.[56] According to the report, Japan's prosperity and dynamism were based on an industrial structure that was deeply dependent on imported oil and other material resources. How was Japan to adjust to the fundamental upheaval in energy and other resource prices that had seriously disturbed the Japanese economy and made many production functions obsolete?

The council concluded that Japan should move from a resources-oriented to a technology-oriented economy, and it recommended a new strategy to meet Japan's future requirements for stabilized development. The technological gap that once existed between Japan and the Western nations had been narrowed through an aggressive industrial strategy. Revolutionary new technologies were drying up throughout the world; Japan should take steps, the council recommended, to acquire a more-independent capacity for R&D. A scientific and technological infrastructure much stronger than Japan possessed should be built through a combination of international cooperation and national effort.

Prime Minister Takeo Fukuda enthusiastically embraced the council's recommendation. He proposed a billion-dollar joint energy program and talked about other large-scale R&D cooperation with the United States and other nations. Before the Diet in 1978, Fukuda declared that "a new era of technological innovation" in Japan would be highlighted by achieving commercialized nuclear fusion in the next twenty years.

Although Fukuda could not get full budgetary backing for his concepts, Japan's policy and strategy are undergoing important shifts in accordance with the analysis and recommendations of the council.[57] The strategy time scale for strengthening the nation's infrastructure has been extended, however. It gives greatest emphasis in the immediate future to product and production-technique improvement. Only marginal increases in government spending for R&D are envisaged.

Economically Japan's intention is to move steadily toward technology-intensive industries, to reduce its vulnerability to volatile resource markets, and to increase its world share of industries having the highest per-capita earnings.[58] High priority is given to computer applications in industry, and a "computerized society" is a primary target for 1990. Technology is to become the foremost marketable product of Japan and a major item for export promotion. Private industry will continue to be the principal source of Japanese technological innovation.

Although technology innovations are the dominant short-term objectives in Japan, a fundamental long-run consensus is moving the nation toward a "science and technology oriented nation through the development of basic science and original technologies."[59] High priority is given to government financing for development of university laboratories and research institutes. A major International Exposition on Science and Technology will be held in Tsukuba Science City in 1985 and will demonstrate Japan's "scientific and technological vision which will make significant contributions to the 21st Century."[60] In short, the Japanese consensus has accepted science and technology as the driving force for the advancement of humanity and has set a national objective for Japan to have a leading global role in offering "human beings a hopeful and vivacious future."

Research for Society in Bonn

Official R&D programs have a long historical tradition in Germany. An intricate institutional infrastructure exists with well-defined roles for federal and state governments, private industry, research laboratories, and universities.[61] It is a decision-shaping structure dominated by a science council in which the business community as well as other relevant interests are represented. The complex machinery for policy and strategy is designed as functioning machinery and is not merely an organizational chart.

An intensive examination of R&D was conducted by the Science Council in the early 1970s, looking for an explanation of Germany's "technological gap" and lagging productivity. The council concluded that more-effective policy machinery should be established and made specific recommendations that had important consequences for German R&D. Public funds are now required to "serve the needs of the state," a view reflected in Chancellor Helmut Schmidt's statement that "research which is financed by society should be obliged to society." The council's finding also resulted in larger federal funding. A government plan is prepared every five years and revised annually, setting forth the objectives of Germany's R&D program and providing approximate budgetary allocations for them.

Private funding remains the principal source of R&D in Germany. Of approximately $11 billion expenditures in 1977, 44 percent was provided by the federal government, compared to more than 50 percent in the United States. Industry's role has an important historical base, particularly in the chemical, pharmaceutical, and optical fields and in the steel and electrical-equipment industries. Industry's ties with universities are extensive and traditional, and for some basic research, such as in chemistry and optics, the private sector is the predominant source of support.

The industrial role is strongly supported by government policy. A 10 percent investment bonus is given for investments in R&D, beyond the general tax and duty deductions for all investments. All current expenses for R&D can be deducted before taxes are calculated. Direct grants are available for research in the public interest when a firm would be competitively injured by making the expenditure on its own. Risk funds are made easier to obtain through government-supported venture-capital banks and through loan guarantees.

Requirements on domestic content of industrial production are imposed to support the development of high-technology industry. Legislation that went into effect in 1981 prohibits international leased communication lines from coming into Germany unless they terminate in a single computer system. Before data or information coming from outside sources—banks, airlines, or financial institutions, for example—can be distributed, they must undergo substantial data processing within Germany. The effect of these requirements on domestic content is to increase installations of data-processing equipment within Germany, thus strengthening internal industry and enlarging the labor-force base in this high-technology industry that Germany wants to develop.

Because of the strength of private-sector R&D, the federal government takes a lesser role in direct subsidization of R&D. Basic research is a significant item of federal support, amounting to about $2.5 billion in 1977. Other support is allocated for targeted objectives, with priority given to high-technology areas where competition from the United States and other advanced nations is stiffest. Computers and data processing have had top priority for many years.

Bonn's support for specific industrial firms has been instrumental in the development of several specific computer and data-processing targets. It enabled AEG-Telefunken and Nixdorf to develop large-size computer production to competitive status, so that both companies are exporting their equipment to the United States.[62] Software AG International is a U.S. subsidiary of Software AG of Darmstadt and is currently expanding its operations in the United States with a $33 million share offering to prospective investors.[63] Software AG is marketing a data-base management system developed with the support of federal subsidies. Other German companies that currently are looking into new applications for computers and data processing are favored recipients of federal funding.

L'Age d'Informatique

In the past decade, no government has exerted greater effort than France to employ R&D policy effectively. Former President Giscard d'Estaing regarded R&D as a logical extension of Gaullist policies of building nationally independent capabilities in critical areas. France has measurably improved its commercial position in communications, aerospace, computers, data communications, and nuclear power and has had the most dynamic economy in Europe. The technological capacities of France were also employed skillfully for political and diplomatic purposes, both in Eastern Europe and in the Third World.

The framework for R&D is an interministerial structure, with individual ministries responsible for R&D in their spheres and advisory committees providing professional scientific input.[64] A major responsibility of the Ministerial Council is the preparation of a national R&D plan that is integrated into the national economic plan.[65] Although no ministry has overall responsibility for R&D and expenditures are channeled through individual ministries, the Interministerial Council is expected to coordinate governmental R&D policies. The structure is one that former President d'Estaing was able to use effectively.

The efforts of a politically and commercially oriented regime brought about substantial changes in commercial high technology. A major white paper commissioned by the president on the "information age" in 1978 was the key to rejuvenating French technological progress.[66] The Nora-Minc report analyzed future economic and technical trends against current conditions in France and concluded that the mastery of information technology was essential to maintain the nation's traditionally independent role. Without an independent capability, France would fall behind. R&D should be stepped up, the report recommended, beginning with telecommunications, computers, data processing, and space and should lead ultimately to technological applications in all industries.[67]

The Nora-Minc recommendations were incorporated in presidential decisions in 1979 designed to undertake a major revival of industrial innovation in France. The Ministry of Industry was overhauled to make it more responsive to international competition. Although initially intended to cope with the U.S. domination of information technology, the policy has a secondary objective of responding to the rising inflow of industrial products from the Third World. This, Ministry of Industry officials explain, is the reason why the program is urging the use of robotics and automation in manufacturing plants of all regions and the country.[68]

Among the principal industrial nations, France relies less than others on private-sector funding for R&D—about 41 percent compared to 44 percent in the United States and nearly 60 percent in Japan. This is partly a reflection of the number of major enterprises that are publicly owned. Tax incentives for private R&D are not particularly generous. In addition, partly-public enterprises apparently receive a significant share of subsidy support from the French treasury.

The Agence Nationale de Valorisation de la Recherche (ANVAR) is an important channel of direct subsidy support. It offers help for companies and firms that are in difficulty because of international competition and want to introduce new production techniques and processes. ANVAR also oversees a special fund for guaranteed bank loans, part of it available for venture capital. About $100 million a year is allocated for the ANVAR program.[69]

The principal effort of the French innovation policy has been an advance in high-technology capability. The Centre Nationale d'Etude Spatiale has made good progress in giving France an independent launching capability for satellite research, remote sensing, and communications. Support for the VLSI circuit programs of CSF-Thomson has been expanded, as well as for the Honeywell-Bull combine for main frame and medium-size computer production. Software service organizations and the telecommunication monopoly have been assisted by direct subsidies as well as by restraints placed on foreign suppliers of such services in France. R&D on integrated circuits using computer-assisted design and manufacture have been made more effective through laboratory mergers brought about by the interventions of the Ministry of Industry.

The Mitterrand government promises to continue and expand its predecessor's emphasis on high technology. Upon assuming the reins of government, it moved with alacrity to begin filling French technology gaps in such fields as microelectronics, biotechnology, and industrial robots. The newly created Ministry of Research and Technology is coordinating the work of scattered research facilities to strengthen the French export effort in technologically advanced products.

U.S. Strategy: A Program in Search of a Purpose

R&D policy in the United States pursues many different objectives. U.S. policy is less systematically related to national commercial and trade objectives than are the policies of its principal technological competitors. Overall policy for industrial R&D is loosely conceived, in keeping with beliefs in scientific freedom and the efficacy of the marketplace. In principle, the United States places strong reliance on private-sector initiatives to determine the size and content of the overall commercial effort. In practice, the large federal outlays on R&D combined with the sweeping influences of the federal government over private resource and investment decisions dilute the role of private initiative far more than the common mythology acknowledges.

Government money represents a larger part of total R&D expenditures in the United States than does government money in any other major industrial nation; yet federal influence, even apart from its emphasis on basic research, has not exercised well-defined commercial objectives or conducted a clearly articulated economic and technological strategy. The federal budget does not include a distinct R&D component. Even more than other elements of the federal establishment, R&D is conducted as a widely diffused government function. Major official programs are born, flourish, and mature with minimum interagency coherence. With rare exception, only perfunctory reference is given to international commercial implications. Projects sometimes take on a life of their own and proceed with little regard to commercial considerations.

Federal influence also has a confounding effect on commercial R&D when government priorities shift unpredictably. It takes time and therefore money to build an effective research team of individual scientists working together harmoniously and productively. When priorities change, the scientific specialties required shift, and a new team must be put together; productivity will decline at least temporarily, but for a significant period. Changes in priority that affect international R&D collaboration, moreover, create unnecessary frictions and are politically disruptive. During the 1970s, priorities changed dramatically many times—from national defense to environment, to fighting inflation, and back again to national defense. The recurrent upheavals have been disruptive to an industrial R&D community that performs the work and has to move from half-completed research projects to those that are hastily conceived. The spin-off effects of federal R&D have been greatly reduced; indeed one perceptive observer has pointed out that defense R&D today is borrowing technology from private industry instead of lending it.[70]

One important consequence of the lack of direction of federal policy has been a gradual shift downward of federal support for industrial R&D. As table 3-7 shows, federal allocations for industrial R&D have not been maintained at levels that keep up with the inflation of the 1970s. By 1980 real federal outlays were only 65 percent of earlier levels and probably fell further in 1981. U.S. industry has had to face external competition with a double handicap from the federal government: flagging funding support and inconstant and commercially disruptive priorities.

Several attempts have been made to bring about more-rational policy-

Table 3-7
U.S. Industrial R&D, 1967-1980
(billions of 1972 dollars)

Source of Funds	1967	1972	1979	1980
Federal government	11.51	8.02	7.48	7.45
Industry	11.04	11.53	15.31	15.80
Total	22.55	19.55	22.79	23.26[a]

Source: National Science Foundation, *National Patterns of Research and Development Resources, 1953-79;* American Association for the Advancement of Science, *Research and Development Report VI,* AAAS, Washington, D.C., 1981. These data differ in some respects from the OECD collated data.
[a]Numbers have been rounded so totals may not equal the sum of components.

making in science and technology. The National Science Foundation, established in 1950, has strengthened the science community significantly by defining and supporting basic research objectives. Important steps have been taken in the appointment since the early 1950s of a science adviser to the president and the establishment in 1974 of the Office of Scientific and Technological Policy, which the science adviser heads.

Primary attention of the science adviser has been given to scientific considerations rather than to commercial technology. In the late 1970s, however, the science adviser and the secretary of commerce collaborated on an important study of industrial innovations, looking into the links between research and commercial innovations and into government policies that might strengthen U.S. competitiveness.[71] The report was a collaborative effort between the government and the private sector, though the final action recommendations were screened by the executive office staff. The report was released in a presidential message in 1979. It emphasized two important obstacles to industrial innovation: excessive regulation and insufficient financial resources available for innovation. Steps recommended to deal with these obstacles were a combination of federal incentives for encouraging private R&D and federal programs to assist private industry to relate R&D more closely to commercially useful activity.

Very few of the recommendations of the industrial innovation study have been carried out. Despite the urgency expressed in the report, only a few of the federal programs were initiated in 1980, and the incentives program had not been enacted when the Carter administration left office. Budgetary allocations requested in the FY 1982 budget for the program were eliminated by the Reagan administration. In addition, staff members assigned for the innovation-support program were transferred and the offices disbanded.

The R&D policies of the Reagan administration have favored greater reliance on private-industry R&D and more concentration of federal R&D in defensive areas. The president's science adviser, George Keyworth, has placed particular stress on making "hard choices" in order to allocate reduced funding in areas of "maximum promise and clear relevancy." He and other administration officials have described specific views favoring tighter controls over federal spending for civilian R&D; reliance on private industry for demonstration and development and greater concentration of federal support for basic research; tax incentives to release industrial funding for R&D; deregulation to release talent and capital for productive R&D; and increased defense R&D.[72]

Some action has been taken on several of these points. In particular, the administration's tax bill provided for general business tax reductions that will release funds that can be used for R&D. Moreover, the bill provided for a 25 percent tax credit for incremental spending on R&D personnel.

These general attitudes are reflected in the budgets for FY 1981 and FY 1982, summarized in table 3-8, and in administration proposals for FY 1983. Thus, in two years' time, defense R&D will increase almost $9 billion. In that period, nondefense expenditures will rise about $600 million, which will likely represent a real reduction when account is taken of anticipated price increases. Several specific steps taken in the budget-revision process may be noted. For example, much of the energy program, particularly solar and coal research, has been drastically curtailed, although nuclear-energy research has been substantially increased. Funds for several international research projects in which the United States has expected to participate have been cut from the budget.

This is a critical period in R&D policy, and the administration's R&D programs have been criticized as inadequate. Many members of the scientific community believe that much more federal support is needed in basic research and in particular fields such as space science, energy, and social-science research. The strongest complaints are voiced against reductions in student support and graduate training in universities, which, it is charged, will lead to deficiencies and shortages of engineers, scientists, and professional research personnel in the future. It remains to be seen, however, whether the new approach will work; it remains to be proven that restraint on federally funded civilian R&D will be matched by privately funded R&D efforts vigorous enough to counter the foreign threat to U.S. technological leadership.

Bold and imaginative policies will be required if the Reagan administration's approach is to reverse this trend. The United States may be "coasting on earlier gains," as the head of the American Productivity Center claims, and not as the conventional wisdom asserts, employing R&D as the cutting edge for an advancing economy.[73] Unless effective steps are taken, the comparative position of the United States will continue to deteriorate. Its com-

Table 3–8
Federal Funding for R&D in the United States, 1972–1982
(billions of current U.S. dollars)

Activity	1972[b]	1980[b]	1981[c]	1982[c]	1982[d]
Basic research	2.2	4.7	5.0	5.5	2.6
Applied research	3.6	6.9	7.3	7.9	3.7
Development	10.7	20.0	23.1	27.3	12.9
R&D facilities	0.6	1.5	1.5	1.4	0.7
Total R&D[a]	17.1	33.1	36.9	42.2	19.9
Defense	9.1	15.4	19.0	24.0	11.3
Nondefense	8.0	17.6	17.9	18.2	8.6

Source: American Association for the Advancement of Science, *Research and Development Report VI* (Washington, D.C.: AAAS, 1981).
[a]Numbers have been rounded, so totals may not be equal the sum of components.
[b]Actual expenditures.
[c]Proposed expenditures.
[d]Funding for 1981 calculated at 1972 prices.

petitors have found commercial vulnerabilities in the U.S. technological armor. Many of them are far more formidable adversaries than in the past. The United States can expect further assaults on its technological leadership. It needs to address a national agenda for regaining that leadership.

Today's Agenda for Tomorrow

R&D is carried out in an international environment that has changed over the past quarter-century. Diffusion of new technology has greatly accelerated, and other nations have found commercially effective ways to concentrate their limited resources on technological adaptations. All of the principal competitors of the United States follow policies that are committed to competitive growth and in the past five years have installed new programs for further supporting and stimulating technology innovations. The United States can retain international preeminence only with an expanding level and quality of technological advance and a use of R&D resources that leads the advances of others. If the United States is to restore its technological preeminence, its R&D must be revitalized.

Following are seven important items for beginning the restoration agenda. They are not presented as a program for restoration; they are intended to indicate the direction that discussion might profitably take to establish a restoration program.

1. Energizing corporate R&D. United States corporate R&D faces aggressive and increasingly capable challenges from competitors in the rest of the industrialized world. More-vigorous private R&D is the most effective way to strengthen the commercial technology position of the United States. Although there are limits on measures government can take that will help, the situation requires more than passive federal policy. Two ways the federal government can help are through tax policy and transferring the focus of R&D from federal to private responsibility in several areas.

2. Further tax incentives. Incentives specifically directed at encouraging private-sector high-technology R&D would be helpful. They should be applied as positive measures to improve U.S. production and efficiency and to encourage real product and real service improvements rather than superficial changes that amount to little more than sales stimulation. Some steps in this direction have already been taken. Preliminary evidence, however, suggests a differential impact among industries, which is apparently far from neutral. If the tax incentives for R&D are indeed nonneutral among industries, they should favor those industries of U.S. comparative advantage or at least not be detrimental to them. Extending the tax credit to apply not only to incremental R&D but also to cover a portion of total R&D expenditures, including salaries of scientists, on high-technology products and processes would provide an important additional incentive. Faster write-offs for start-up investments in new high-technology areas would be helpful. A change in the internal revenue code is needed to permit corporations to write off R&D expenses where the expenditures occur rather than in proportion to international sales.

3. Transferring R&D from public to private hands. Ensuring that basic research is adequately supported both privately and publicly is a major social responsibility that can be dealt with only at the federal level. The research itself, however, should be conducted in the private sector, especially in nonprofit institutions and universities. Federal R&D areas, such as defense and public health, are also connected with acquiring fundamental knowledge or with security functions that can be performed only by the federal government. These important and legitimate functions of government should be actively pursued and adequately supported and should not be confused with R&D where private-sector responsibility is more appropriate. The latter is especially the case where judgments about economic feasibility are required. Government R&D could usefully be limited to basic research and to such development and engineering as is directly related to narrowly construed federal functions.

It is equally important to stress what the government should not attempt to do. Decisions concerning those industries that are to be tomorrow's growth industries are much more safely and efficiently made by the market mechanism. Because knowledge is imperfect in the market, the government can support this mechanism by publicizing gaps in R&D,

pointing out areas of R&D that lag or lead, and thus help the market to decide more quickly and efficiently where future growth should occur. Except in emergencies, however, that decision should not be made by the government.

It is also important that solutions to problems of foreign-government interference with the market mechanism (like foreign subsidies to U.S. exporters' competitors) be sought through measures that work with market forces, not against them. The proper (that is, the optimum) solution to foreign subsidies is one that causes international trade in R&D to expand, not to decline. The optimum solution is countersubsidies, not import control. Similarly government support for R&D in the United States should aim at ameliorating market imperfections and helping the market mechanism to work.

4. Confronting competition in the international technology industry. Technology is most often embodied in exported goods and equipment or as an integral part of whole plants constructed abroad. In addition, private-sector technology, apart from the products and services in which it is embodied, is becoming a thriving world industry. Based originally on efforts to improve corporate products and processes, international markets for the sale of such technology are avidly sought because exports add to revenues without commensurate expenses and thus contribute to cost recovery. Recently high-technology service industries, such as computer software and industrial design, have made technology production and sales an end in themselves.

Despite the technological prominence of the United States, government policy on marketing high-technology and high-technology products is ambiguous and constitutes an unnecessary hindrance to American high-technology companies. The federal government's desire to deny strategic technologies to some buyers on security grounds lies behind the ambiguous policies that have cost billions of dollars in exports of hard goods incorporating the technologies—nuclear reactors, computer installations, oil pipe, and satellite rocketry, for example. Unless clarified, the policy will become an increasing hindrance as competitors narrow the remaining gaps between their high technology and that of the United States. An unambiguous and stable policy for the international technology industry would enable U.S. industry to organize itself suitably for competition in what could become the principal international growth industry in the next decade.

5. High technology and the industrially emerging Third World nations. The front-runners among the industrially emerging countries stand today where the United States, Europe, and Japan stood in the 1950s. It is reasonable to expect that in the next two decades, they will be doing what the advanced nations did in the past two: expanding production and inter-

national trade in automobiles, steel, plastics, pharmaceuticals, machine tools, industrial machinery, transport equipment, textiles, petrochemicals, and other medium-technology and heavy-industry products. This is bound to have displacement consequences for the economies in technologically advanced countries and, in turn, will set off production and trade readjustments among the advanced nations.

A main question for the United States concerns the impact of growing Third World competition on domestic production and employment. Adjustment in the United States should take two forms: moving production and jobs into high-technology industries and moving high-technology processes into traditional or middle-technology industries.

A technology-intensive policy based on such a design would enable the United States to improve productivity steadily and at the same time permit a new market-determined balance between domestic production and imports in traditional manufacturing industries. This policy would enable U.S. producers to compete more efficiently with Japanese and Europeans for markets in the United States and in developing countries. A technology policy following these principles would achieve the economic objective of maximizing productivity of U.S. resources and obtaining goods from the cheapest suppliers, as well as the political objective of providing markets for the legitimate development aspirations of the Third World.

6. Improving international cooperation in high-cost science and technology. There are two areas of science and technology where greater international cooperation is warranted: high-cost basic research and social-overhead R&D. In both areas the benefits of new knowledge are shared generally; the costs and risks should also be shared generally. Probes of the solar system, for example, are enormously expensive for U.S. taxpayers; the knowledge gained is disseminated quickly to the rest of the world. Cost sharing is overdue.

The principal advanced nations, moreover, are uneasy about growing evidence that basic sources of technological innovation are drying up and about the impasse posed when expansion of basic knowledge requires R&D expenditures exceeding the resources of individual nations. They have been very cautious in accepting new approaches that require large budgetary commitments; nevertheless, the receptivity in Europe and Japan to cooperative science and technology has gradually warmed in the past five years and could change significantly over the coming decade.

A major shift in attitude is not likely, however, unless the United States takes a leading position in supporting shared participation in R&D. For example, a U.S. policy calling for gradual evolution toward international cooperation in science and technology research on large-scale projects would likely be favorably received and lead in time to a new form of international infrastructure that would serve the interests of all nations. A good place to start is NATO, where cooperative research in basic sciences and in weapons development has been successfully pursued for many years. A second place is in the framework of the United States–Japan science and technology agreements.

Expanded international cooperation for high-cost basic science and technology would produce three benefits for U.S. commercial technology. It would enable basic research to proceed more rapidly than if the United States pursued its own independent course. The stream of new knowledge for application by the private sector in commerical technology would be fuller and surer. Over time international cooperation would ease the burden on U.S. R&D resources, thus enabling the United States to concentrate more effectively on application of new knowledge. Finally, it could diminish the need for exclusive intra-European collaboration that would work against U.S. interests.

7. Strengthening federal policy. Technological strength is an essential element in U.S. global security and international leadership because technology power accentuates and underlines economic and military power. Institutional machinery is needed to ensure the technological preeminence that will serve international security and economic objectives. Existing policy machinery for commercial R&D is not achieving these results.

U.S. technological strength could be restored through a national commitment to the advancement of science and high technology as a major national goal. Machinery for such a commitment could be established through a Council of Technology Advisers. Among its functions would be to draw up a five-year assessment of world and U.S. technological prospects and potentials, to update the assessment each year, and to provide guidance for decision making on technology-policy issues.

American business participation would be an essential element in a Council of Technology Advisers. How much government should lead and how much business should follow can be determined effectively only through a practical dialogue that leads to workable consensus. One of the principal functions of the council would be to establish a useful dialogue between the government and the private sector on R&D, on world needs and U.S. potential, and on innovation policy.

A restoration agenda could bring new life into U.S. export competitiveness. It could restore the technological leadership that sparked three decades of unprecedented economic development and created a new interdependency among nations. A restoration agenda today could become the platform for U.S. leadership in the interdependent world of the last two decades of the twentieth century.

4

Government Support for Exports: The Financing of Exports

Subsidies for export finance became a subject of embittered international dispute among the major industrial countries of the world at the time when interest rates worldwide reached unprecedented levels. Heavy subsidies were the consequence of two forces. First, high interest rates tend to depress economic activity, to contract markets, and thus to make international competition for export markets more intense. Especially when high interest rates coincide with balance-of-payments deficits, as they did in the late 1970s and early 1980s because of high oil prices, governments push exports even more aggressively. Second, high interest rates, by raising the cost of credit, make export finance a larger proportion of the total price of exports and especially of big-ticket items that are paid for over a relatively long term (for example, more than five years). As a consequence, subsidies for export credits take on greater significance in the competition for export markets. If market rates are 20 percent and a private exporters' anticipated profit on a transaction is 7 percent, the exporter will lose money on the entire export transaction if it attempts to offer export financing at less than 17.5 percent for a five-year loan.[1]

Thus the scope for effective alternative forms of government support for export finance depends almost entirely on the level of interest rates in the private sector. If market rates are 15 percent, an exporter expecting to earn 7 percent on an export transaction might be willing to offer export credit at rates of less than 15 percent if it perceives other benefits (in addition to the immediate profit) from winning the order. Similarly an export-financing institution able to acquire funds at less than market rates (for example, a bank that could discount export paper at the Federal Reserve rate or the government borrowing rate) would find its services in greater demand when interest rates are lower than when they are higher. If the difference between the market rate and the discount rate is 5 percent while foreign competitors are getting a 7 to 10 percent subsidy, the U.S. exporter is likely to be out of the race and thus not to seek accommodation directly from the bank or indirectly from the Federal Reserve.

Government support for export finance can assume a variety of forms, ranging from interest-rate subsidies, through preferential discount facilities, insurance for the exporter against various political and commercial risks, to outright guarantees of repayment to the exporter's bank or the exporter. Similarly the amount of government aid provided in the form of preferences or concessions below the market equivalents varies through time and across countries.

Foreign Practice

In general, competitors for U.S. export markets provide official export-finance support through insurance and credit facilities that offer short-, medium-, and long-term export financing.[2] Although most official foreign support has concentrated on long-term (up to ten years) and medium-term financing, recently more effort has been devoted to new techniques for facilities beyond the traditional limit of ten years. Further, official export finance continues to be offered at interest rates that are fixed for the duration of the loan, a practice that has become increasingly infrequent in commercial banking since the onset of highly volatile interest rates in the late 1970s.[3] The provision of long-term fixed-rate financing in an era of highly volatile interest rates is a form of subsidy, for the government assumes the risk of future rate changes and in so doing makes it possible for the buyer to know in advance the total cost of the import. Such certainty is often not possible in private-market long-term financing. In addition, most foreign official export-credit agencies are increasingly making export credits available in currencies other than their own.

Almost all government-finance facilities require that insurance against political and commercial risks be carried on the credits they finance. In most cases they also maintain an insurance facility themselves that provides the necessary coverage for a fee; indeed some systems rely on insurance and guarantees as the main form of government support. Insurance against political risks (war, expropriation, and exchange restrictions, for example) is available only from a limited number of private companies, although many private companies are willing to underwrite insurance against commercial risks—for example, default by the borrower or failure to accept goods. Government financing agencies typically offer both. The interplay between insurance and credit in government support for export finance is very close. In fact, the ready availability of government insurance and guarantees to private banks, made highly liquid by the inflow of petro-dollars and competing for export-financing contracts, may have contributed to a general loosening of bank criteria for credit-worthiness and thus encouraged borrowers to undertake uneconomic projects. Such unfortunate consequences need not follow, however.

In addition to the usual political and commercial risks, several official export-finance agencies have offered additional protection against specified foreign-exchange risks and inflationary price increases. Both France and the United Kingdom, for example, offer partial protection against price increases on capital-goods exports during the production period. The German system offers insurance against inflationary price increases only in the event of an actual loss under commerical or political risk coverage.

The amount of private-sector participation in government programs of export-credit finance varies considerably among countries. In some cases this is a reflection of the degree to which the commercial banking system has been nationalized. Even before the advent of the Mitterrand administration in France, for example, nearly all commercial banks were government owned. In part this participation is a reflection of the scope of the national programs, which ranges from the simple provision of an insurance facility (such limited efforts are mainly confined to LDC export-finance agencies) to the provision of a wide variety of banking and investment services associated with foreign trade by the government facility alone or in collaboration with the private sector (France and Japan, for example). Some government financing agencies have on their boards of directors representatives from private banking, trade, and organized labor (France); others have representatives from the private sector as advisers (Germany's Hermes Kreditversicherung A.G.); still others are entirely government administered (United States and Japan).

Most official export-finance agencies operate under annual budgetary appropriations, although budgets have most commonly been increased by supplementary appropriations when necessary. The French system, which appears to provide an open-ended claim on the French treasury, is the most liberally financed official system. The German system probably involves the lowest level of public support (although comparisons are difficult), and the Export-Import Bank of Japan is said to have grown into the largest government financing institution in the world.[4]

Public funds provide the original source for the bulk of the credit facilities of most official export-finance agencies. Many of them—Japan and Germany, for example—have continuing authority to borrow from the private banking system at home or abroad, but while Japan has never used its authority, Germany has always relied primarily on the private sector. The United States (Eximbank) uses both public and private funds; it borrows the former while the latter is provided primarily by the Private Export Funding Corporation (PEFCO), which sells its own debt obligations at favorable rates on the private market because its assets bear an Eximbank guarantee. The U.S. Eximbank is the only such institution whose current activities are constrained by the necessity to use only its own resources.

The official export-credit agencies of France, the United Kingdom, and Germany make special provision for national-interest transactions in addition to normal commerical transactions. National-interest transactions are those that the government wishes to encourage for domestic as well as foreign political reasons, or for economic reasons but that in most cases would not be undertaken without official intervention. The concept appears to be a highly elastic one that includes both meeting foreign competition and serving narrowly defined foreign-policy goals. Further, it seems likely that most official export-finance agencies informally make provisions, as required by pressure from the foreign office, for "political" loans. Japanese and German loans to financially weak but strategically important countries like Pakistan and Poland are examples.

Government support for export finance originally took the form of a direct guarantee to commercial banks making export loans on capital goods during the early postwar years when pervasive foreign-exchange shortages around the world made such loans risky. Guarantees were later supplemented by government facilities to refinance export credits in order to alleviate shortages of domestic liquidity. Intensifying competition for export markets led to subsidies for interest rates and to increasingly generous forms of government support such as insurance against losses due to production cost increases and exchange-rate fluctuations. In the late 1970s subsidies to export finance in the form of mixed credits—a combination of the standard export credit and foreign aid—became the most aggressively competitive instrument of government support.

The International Agreement

The heightened intensity of export-credit competition led OECD countries in 1976 to agree informally to apply the same credit terms (rates, down payment, and maturity) according to certain classes of buyers. These "consensus guidelines" were incorporated in 1978 in the OECD-sponsored Arrangement on Guidelines for Officially Supported Export Credit. Subsequently, however, while the Arrangement rates remained fixed and uniform for all currencies, market interest rates rose dramatically, but by different amounts in different countries. In an effort to bring order into the increasing chaos, the Arrangement countries in 1979 established a study group (under the Swedish banker, Axel Wallen) charged with recommending alternatives for coping with the changed circumstances. Despite a prompt report from this group recommending three alternatives, no new consensus was possible.

In October 1981 after prolonged negotiations, many threats, and much cajoling, the member countries agreed to raise minimum export-credit rates by 2.25 to 2.5 percentage points. The existing range of interest rates, which varied from 7.5 to 8.75 percent (depending on the affluence of the borrowing country and the maturity term), was raised to a range of 10.0 percent to 11.25 percent. A floor of 9.25 percent was also set for low-interest countries in which internal market rates may be below the agreement floor. In addition, an agreement with West Germany, France, and the United Kingdom was concluded on the financing of exports of larger commercial aircraft. It contained a minimum U.S. dollar interest rate of 12 percent, a maximum of ten years for the credit term, direct credit support of 62.5 percent or 42.5 percent depending on the repayment schedules of private and official financing, and limits on the amount of official financial support to be offered for spare parts.[5]

These are, of course, moves in the right direction, albeit modest and very marginal in the context of subsidies in the vicinity of 8 to 10 percentage points. They reduced the level of the subsidy, but only to that prevailing in June 1980, and left the minimum rates below even the World Bank rates to LDCs. The agreements were not achieved without costs to the United States, which either abandoned or prolonged its efforts to lengthen terms, especially for aircraft credits, to beyond ten years. Because the United States clearly has a strong comparative advantage in long-term credit markets, this was an important concession that may have been bargained away for too low a return. In short, the intensity of the international competition in export finance continues unabated, especially in its most virulent form—mixed credits.

According to the international Arrangement, a mixed credit is an export credit with a grant element of less than 25 percent. Some claim that it is accepted by the Arrangement (although not necessarily by the GATT) provided the standard part of the credit is at the consensus rates. (A similar mixing of aid funds with commercial lending is referred to as parallel financing. It is not subject to reporting according to the terms of the Arrangement.) The Arrangement requires prior notification of at least ten calendar days of intention to use a mixed credit with an aid element of less than 15 percent. If the aid element is 15 to 20 percent, notice must be given at the time the commitment is entered into. There is widespread criticism that these prenotification requirements are much too short to permit a matching offer by a competitor. A blending of standard and aid credits where the aid component is more than 25 percent of the total is not mentioned in the Arrangement, which thereby defines foreign aid (or official development assistance) as any credit with a concessional element of at least one-quarter of the total. This practice accepts the definition of foreign aid used by OECD's Development Assistance Committee (DAC).

Mixed Credits

In a fiercely competitive environment, the great advantage of mixed credits is that they permit a more-attractive package of financing terms than that allowed under the guidelines, while still being within the guidelines. Their virulence stems from the fact that they encourage the LDCs to play off one exporter against another. Insofar as exporters have appropriated funds for use as mixed credits, which they would not otherwise have appropriated for their development-assistance programs, this practice has served to increase the total amount of aid available to the LDCs.

Britain, for example, budgeted £2 million ($4.6 million) for the grant element of its mixed credits in 1981 and $9.2 million for 1982. The Canadian government recently established a (C)$900 million mixed credit facility for 1982 through 1984. In the winter of 1981, Japan announced a new policy of intent to match mixed credits whenever Japanese exporters of complete plants encountered them as competition. Norway, Sweden, and the Netherlands have also announced mixed-credit facilities. Not all of these represent net additions to development-assistance programs, but it seems likely that, in the aggregate, mixed-credit implementation has increased aid availability.

Japan, like Britain, mixes export credits and aid funds in such a way that the grant element is close to, but above, 25 percent and thus outside the guidelines. In each country the grant element is provided by the aid agency and thus must meet the criteria for aid, but there are always exceptions. Japan's aid budget has more than doubled in the past three years, bringing it into third place in the list of donor countries within the DAC (which ranks aid programs in relation to their GNP). In January 1981 the Japanese prime minister announced that Japan's foreign aid for the years 1981–1985 would amount to $21.4 billion. Japan is thus well positioned to join the mixed-credit competitive fray.

Competition among donors of foreign aid is an outcome not entirely to be deplored. Public-aid expenditures can be justified on grounds of national security as well as on grounds of philanthropy. A U.S. policy of using mixed credits to match foreign-government subsidies of their exports of goods and services in which the United States has a strong comparative advantage would thus yield an additional benefit to U.S. aid expenditures: the productivity benefit, which is the consequence of inhibiting the misallocation of U.S. resources that would otherwise occur. Further, since foreign-aid appropriations have proven to be notoriously difficult to get through Congress, international competition in foreign aid might serve to make the Congress more amenable to requests for aid funds.

This last point should not be overstressed. For the poorest of the developing countries, imports of capital goods and equipment embodying the most-advanced technology are often not appropriate. Economies with a surplus of unskilled labor and a paucity of trained people in all fields are rarely candidates for sophisticated labor-saving machinery. Nonetheless, these countries do require power plants, jet aircraft, and such high-technology items for their infrastructures, and consequently there are cases where mixed credits are economically justifiable. For the more-advanced newly industrializing countries that no longer are aid recipients, U.S. countersubsidies are justifiable only in terms of neutralizing foreign competition. In these cases, mixed credits are not the optimum form of countersubsidy if U.S. aid funds are scarce. The United States initiated a mixed-credit undertaking at the start of the 1980s with a loan to Egypt that combined Eximbank funds with aid monies. Unless the resources of both agencies are expanded in the future, such efforts by the United States must remain highly selective and small. Any U.S. program of mixed credits should require that the exports being so financed meet the development criteria of the U.S. aid agency.[6]

It is worth repeating that the form of the export subsidy is less important than its size and flexibility. Foreign aid by its nature is a subsidy to the donor's export industries, whether or not aid is tied. Many, if not most, U.S. competitors for international markets view their aid expenditures as justified on grounds of maintaining and expanding their export markets in developing countries. In fact, more than 55 percent of the bilateral aid of OECD countries goes to middle-income countries where less than 30 percent of the Third World's populations live.[7] Foreign aid, whether by itself or blended with government support or with private-sector credits into various forms of export finance, is a subsidy to exports. It should, when appropriate, be perceived as one of the instruments available for U.S. government support in maintaining at strength its industries of comparative advantage.

The Present Environment

In the past decade cooperation between the public and private sectors has produced a wealth of new forms of finance to cope with changing circumstances in the domestic economy. New instruments and new techniques have emerged to facilitate the financing of housing, industrial and commercial construction, machinery and equipment, and new ventures. Freddie Macs (issues of the Federal Home Loan Mortgage Corporation), industrial-revenue bonds, equipment leases, and venture-capital funds are innovations supported by the government through some form of tax or interest-rate concession. (Venture-capital funds, for example, received a big boost from the 1978 reduction of the capital-gains tax.) Similarly, new instruments have facilitated the mobilization of savings from individuals and corporations (the money-market funds, for example).

Until very recently, such broad-scale, innovative activity has been almost totally absent from the field of export finance. New ideas for a public and private cooperative effort in export finance are beginning to emerge in the private sector and are deserving of at least the same degree of government acquiescence and support as the earlier efforts in domestic finance. This is true because of the importance of exports in U.S. economic revitalization and because of the lack of flexibility that has characterized U.S. export finance in the face of increasingly flexible and innovative developments abroad.[8]

Suggestions for supplementing or expanding the facilities of the Eximbank to support U.S. exports derive from complaints about the availability of funds at rates of interest that are internationally competitive. The shortage of export funding at competitive rates is the result of two factors over which the United States has little control and of one factor within its control.

Subsidies to export finance by foreign governments have been only marginally amenable to U.S. influence. It is these foreign subsidies that in part make U.S. export finance, which is mostly tied to market rates, noncompetitive. In addition, market interest rates prevailing within industrial countries can diverge markedly; this divergence reflects primarily differing fiscal and monetary policies among countries that themselves are responses to nonsynchronized national business cycles and widely divergent structural conditions among national economies. The higher the general level of interest rates worldwide, moreover, the greater the opportunity for seriously disruptive interest-rate differentials. Over the past decade, Japan and Germany have been low-inflation-rate countries. Their exporters have been able to compete in world markets with little or no subsidy to export finance in part because of their low market rates of interest and in part because of the existence of other forms of subsidy to exports. As competition has mounted in intensity, however, even Japan and Germany have been forced into more subsidization of export finance.

In the United States, the shortage of finance at competitive rates has been the consequence of limited authorizations of funds for Eximbank's discount-loan and direct-loan programs and of congressional resistance to increasing the contingent liability of the United States (for example, through the use of government guarantees). The amount of subsidy involved in the discount-loan program, for example, has been limited to the difference between market rates and the Federal Reserve discount rate, which has been not insignificant but not nearly a match for the rates available to competitors in countries like the United Kingdom or France.

The subsidy involved in the direct-loan program has been limited primarily by the Eximbank tradition (not congressionally mandated) of being a self-supporting institution. As long as U.S. market interest rates were relatively low, this tradition was not a constraint, but it became a serious one in the late 1970s when U.S. market rates soared. It is important that the U.S. Congress remove this constraint by confirming that Eximbank's mission is to provide export finance at competitive rates (which existing legislation does), not to make a profit. As the Government Accounting Office (GAO) has pointed out, the two goals are mutually exclusive.[9] The perceived requirement to be self-supporting together with increasing demands for Eximbank accommodation at competitive rates (as more and more U.S. exporters had to seek low-cost credit to compete) has created an acute shortage of Eximbank resources, which has been accentuated by the impact of inflation in the face of authorizations that failed to keep pace. The U.S. Eximbank is the only such institution using its own resources to support current operations.

Congressional concern over the mounting gross value of contingent liabilities seems misplaced. What is relevant is the direct burden on the U.S. Treasury, that is, the loss rate. Actual losses are controllable by maintaining standards of credit-worthiness, although situations where losses arise from revolutions or coups d'etats (Iran, for example) are almost impossible to foresee. In fact, guarantees and insurance are a source of income to the government from the fees and premiums involved. Thus far Eximbank has earned more from PEFCO fees than it has paid out on PEFCO loan defaults.

Basically government support for export finance takes one, or both, of two forms: an interest-rate subsidy or a tax benefit. Possible variations of each of these two forms are extensive. One important form of interest-rate subsidy, for example, is a government guarantee of the promissory note of the buyer or the supplier. Because the government guarantees the interest and principal payments of the private-sector borrower and because the risk involved in lending to the U.S. government is perceived as less than that entailed in lending to a private business or another sovereign nation, the interest charged is lower than the market would be willing to grant without the guarantee. In assuming the ultimate risk, the government in effect subsidizes the interest rate on the loan. Similarly, in guaranteeing private export credits against political and commercial risks, the government makes possible a lower interest charge from the banks. Further, the dividing line between interest subsidy and a tax benefit is by no means clearly defined. A tax-free bond issue, for example, can be seen as either a tax benefit or an interest-rate subsidy.

The balance of this chapter discusses various forms of additional government support for export finance according to whether they use existing institutions and instruments or require the creation of new institutions or instruments of trade finance. This discussion is neither thorough nor complete. There are many actors on the scene offering proposals on intricate matters. The proposals are not always in written form, most often not in published form. Rather they exist in correspondence, in internal corporate or government memoranda, in minutes of meetings, and in conversations. Some of the proposals have been worked out in detail; others contain only

the germ of an idea. There is no way of ascertaining where the idea originated or whether all proposals that have been mentioned somewhere have
been covered. Thus the proposals here are discussed in general terms and
should be perceived as representing the types of ideas for coping with the
problems of export finance that are circulating among concerned people.

Expanding the Resources of Existing Institutions

Administratively, the simplest form of expanded U.S. government support
for export finance would lie in increasing the resources available to the
Eximbank. A wide array of business persons, bankers, private consultants,
and academicians recently has importuned the Congress and the executive
branch to do just this.

Such advice from the private sector has not been unanimous. Those
opposing such support for U.S. exports, however, usually have based their
objections explicitly or implicitly on the mistaken notion that a dollar's
worth of exports adds no more to GNP than a dollar's worth of output for
the domestic market.[10] If one accepts the elementary concept that a division
of labor (specialization and exchange) increases productivity and that specialization is limited by the size of the market, it follows that, on the average, production for export enhances the productivity of all of a country's
productive resources. Most critics have ignored this basic verity, stated as
far back as 1776 by Adam Smith.

It is not necessary here to review the reasons for expanding all of Eximbank's programs—the direct-loan fund, the discount-loan capacity, the
guarantee and insurance programs—and for ameliorating the general lack
of flexibility within programs. The inadequacies have been well documented
in articles and congressional testimony.[11] They are constraining in all of the
realms in which Eximbank operates. They exist in resources available for
supporting smaller exporters or contracts of less than $5 million, or those
requiring medium-term financing (of less than five years), as well as on
those big-ticket items requiring long-term, larger-scale financing. They also
exist in the bank's guarantee program and in its insurance programs. The
remedies suggested similarly range across the spectrum of the bank's activities and beyond.

Among exporters and commercial banks, it is widely believed that
increased flexibility in Eximbank's operations is as necessary as increased
resources. Each commercial bank operates within its own policy objectives
and under constraints that vary considerably from bank to bank. Adjusting
existing Eximbank programs to recognize some of these individual differences among banks would aid in making the bank more competitive. The
assessment of risk in a given contract is likely to vary considerably among

banks depending on their individual circumstances and preconceptions, for example. As a consequence one bank may be willing to accept a larger amount of commercial or political risk for a short period but will not accept even a much smaller degree of risk for a period only a year or two longer. Another bank will be willing to take the same degree of risk for a longer period. If Eximbank were to adjust its standard guarantee to provide greater commercial risk coverage in the later years of a given loan in exchange for lesser coverage in the earlier years, the individual requirement of more banks could be satisfied.

Eximbank has in fact been varying its programs in recent years to meet the diverse requirements of its customers. Among its more-recent innovations are its lease guarantees (of questionable operational significance), guarantees of foreign-currency loans, financing for feasibility and planning studies, and guarantees for political risks of equipment used by U.S. contractors abroad. It is clear that relatively minor Eximbank participation in an export-financing transaction can have ripple effects. The existence of Eximbank's guarantees and insurance provided to individual banks, for example, has induced considerable co-lending without such a guarantee for other banks, which would not have occurred without some Eximbank participation in the transaction. Further progress in this direction should be encouraged.

A number of critics have suggested that a general increase in the resources of the Eximbank be achieved by introducing private-sector participation in the bank's ownership. Thus, equity in the bank would be held not only by the U.S. Treasury but also by its customers who, in buying stock in the bank, would contribute to its capital base. Users of the bank would be represented on the board of directors and consequently would have a vote in management and policy.

Such proposals would be fully effective in practice, however, only if the Eximbank does not operate at a loss. In periods of high interest rates and heavy foreign subsidies to export finance, Eximbank loans can be competitive only if they are subsidized. If Eximbank loans are competitive, the bank loses money; if they are not competitive, the bank loses money; if they are not competitive, accommodation will not be sought by its customers, and the bank will not be effective. The private sector, however, does not need to invest in a financial institution if, by itself, it has the resources necessary to subsidize export finance. The proposal, therefore, has operational significance mainly for normal times, but those days may be long delayed in their reappearance. Unless accompanied by an expression of congressional support for loss operations when necessary, making Eximbank a public-private institution would in effect expand its resources when they are least needed—for example, when U.S. market rates are internationally competitive and the bank can operate at a profit.

Even during periods of high interest rates and heavy foreign subsidies, however, the demand for those parts of Eximbank's services that do not involve a loss (such as the discount loan or guarantee programs) can increase, and have done so. Thus an expansion of the bank's resources would be useful for these programs even during periods of heavy foreign subsidies. Because these operations are not a burden on the U.S. Treasury (or need not be), they can be expanded without cost to taxpayers.

If private capital could be attracted to participation in the bank's ownership, by, say, the sale of preferred stock to the private sector, it seems likely that the bank would benefit from the participation on its board of people directly concerned with the intricacies of international finance. It is a dynamic area of rapid change and has become "an increasingly complicated business requiring sophisticated financial expertise."[12] The flexibility of the bank's operations could benefit from the counsel of those who are actively engaged in day-to-day market operations.

Sale of preferred stock by the bank to the private sector would add to the bank's fixed costs, although presumably its customers would be willing to accept a relatively low yield because of the benefits they derive from the bank's total services.[13] The expanded capital base would permit the bank to increase its nonloss services and thus would result in expanded, if limited, accommodation for exporters even during periods of heavy subsidies.

One sizable advantage to making Eximbank a private-public corporation would lie in the fact that such a change in the basic funding of the bank would likely cause it to be removed from the unified federal budget. Because the United States does not follow the practice of many other countries in using a two-part budget encompassing a current budget and a capital budget, it is forced to treat a loan operation like that of Eximbank as if any annual net outflow of funds is an expenditure, although that outflow will be self-liquidating and will be mostly—in the past has been fully—returned to the bank in a future year.

A balance of receipts and expenditures over a time interval longer than twelve months is properly handled in a capital budget. Over its lifetime Eximbank's aggregate receipts have been greater than its aggregate expenditures. Very frequently, however, its annual outflow of funds has been greater than its inflow, with the net outflow being treated as a drain on the U.S. Treasury. In fact, it was a reflection of the use of an inappropriate budgetary time frame.

The U.S. budget per se contains not only net cost outlays but also authorization levels for various Eximbank programs. Authorization makes a loan, guarantee, or insurance available; disbursement follows over a period of years. The impact of the budget on the U.S. Treasury is therefore very different from the authorization levels. The gross cash outflows involved in the direct-loan program came closest to authorizations. The disbursements involved in the contingent liabilities—the guarantees and insurance programs—are only a small fraction of the authorization levels because most of the guarantees and insurance never have to be exercised. In every program, continuing cash receipts mean that the net flow is very different from the gross cash outflow and frequently is positive.

Before 1968 Eximbank funding was not included in the federal budget. Since that time a tale has circulated in Washington that the bank was put into the budget in 1968 only because its prospective cash flow for that year was expected to be positive and thus would appear to reduce somewhat the size of the prospective federal deficit. In view of the pressures that existed then to keep the federal deficit down in the face of the Vietnam buildup, the tale may not be apocryphal. Whether the bank's operations should be in the budget at all is a question meriting serious examination.

Another suggestion for expanding the capital base of Eximbank's operations would give the bank the ability to issue tax-free bonds. Because the income would not be subject to U.S. income taxes, the bonds would be salable at relatively low rates and thus would be a relatively inexpensive means of acquiring additional funds.

Between 1968 and the establishment of the Federal Financing Bank in 1974, the bank did obtain some funds by selling bonds in the private sector. These bonds were subject to the federal income tax but were exempted by some states from income taxes. The Export-Import Bank Act neither authorizes nor prohibits the bank from selling bonds to the private sector. The legislation, however, in specifying that the bank may spend only up to those limits authorized by the Congress effectively curtails the use of this source of funding.

Tax-free bonds would add to the bank's fixed costs, but whether the new funds would be cheap enough to permit the bank to compete would depend on the level of interest rates and the size of foreign subsidies. It seems unlikely that the difference between market rates and yields on such tax-free bonds would approach the 8 to 10 percentage points of foreign subsidies prevailing in 1981. Under these conditions, such an expansion of the bank's resources could help but would not fully solve the problem of meeting foreign competition.

All of the suggestions for expanding Eximbank's resources by tapping the private capital market would require legislation to amend the bank's charter. They would offer a solution to the bank's basic financing problem only under favorable conditions of foreign competition, unless the Congress were willing to vote and the administration willing to use the funds necessary to meet foreign subsidized competition to the exports of industries in which the United States has a clear comparative advantage.

Widespread in the business community is the opinion that Eximbank facilities for offering competitive, fixed-rate, medium-term financing are woefully inadequate and have become increasingly so as interest rates have become higher and more volatile. The discount loan program has been limited to export contracts no larger than $5 million (a maximum that has shrunk considerably in real value since 1979 when it was introduced), and recently the minimum discount was pegged to that of the New York Federal Reserve Bank, which in conditions of 1981 is not internationally competitive.[14]

The discount loan program was conceived as a means of guaranteeing that commercial banks granting export credits would not be put at a disadvantage during periods of liquidity tightness because of heavy export financing. A discount loan is a standby commitment on the part of the Eximbank to provide fixed-rate funding if the commercial bank should so request. Until recently, actual disbursements by the bank under this program have been only a fraction of commitments; the recent institution of a commitment fee has meant that commitments and disbursements are now much closer. Eximbank has always had full recourse on the lending commercial bank.

Several times in recent years, as a means of increasing the resources of the discount loan program, the business community has suggested that the Federal Reserve System accept export paper for rediscounting. Such a facility, if it existed, would make funds available to commercial banks for purposes of financing exports at about the cost of money to the U.S. Treasury and thus would be of some aid in helping to meet foreign competition. Such a facility, however, would require legislation to enlarge the existing basic ninety-day maturity limitation on Federal Reserve discounts.

Such a proposal has been considered several times in the recent past. It has been opposed by the staff of the Federal Reserve Board on the grounds that the Fed does not have any special facilities for individual sectors of the economy. To grant one exception would subject the system to undesirable pressures to extend exceptions to other worthy causes. The result could be a general loosening of requirements for access to Federal Reserve credits and more difficulties for the system in operating an effective monetary policy. This suggestion seems no more likely to be accepted today than it was in the past.

More ominously, for reasons that are difficult to comprehend, the Office of Management and Budget for nearly a decade has sought to abolish the discount-loan program. The danger that this long-standing budgetary goal will be realized is perhaps greater in the early 1980s than ever before. Given the inadequate availability of medium-term, fixed-rate, competitive export funding, the loss of the discount-loan program would be a serious blow to U.S. export efforts. In a world environment that is forcing serious distortion of resource allocation on the U.S. economy and adding to other factors that depress U.S. productivity, more rather than less export finance should be made available to further the national interest.

New Institutions to Finance Exports

Accommodating business requirements for export finance within the private sector is primarily the province of the large city banks along the U.S. coasts and the Great Lakes. Smaller interior regional and local banks serving smaller businesses are little concerned with foreign commerce because their clients are primarily domestic. Increasing the awareness of these banks and their customers to the potential for profits in the export market is part of the export-promotion program of the United States government—and a chicken and egg situation. If the smaller businesses required export finance, their bankers would be more accommodating; if the regional banks were more aware of the profits to be earned in financing international trade, they would be more likely to alert their customers to export opportunities.

Regional banks have not supported or have opposed additional government support for export finance because they perceive no benefit in it for themselves. One reason for this perception lies in the fact that the United States has relied less on the services of commercial banks with country-wide offices than have other countries in their official export-finance mechanisms. U.S. reliance on Eximbank's Washington office has limited its services to those exporters with the personnel and skills available to work with and in Washington. If full advantage were taken of the regional banks, more export finance could be made available to small exporters.

Another reason for the perception of regional banks—that they do not benefit from government support for export finance—lies in the very limited facilities of the Eximbank for supporting fixed-rate, medium-term contracts or export contracts of less than $5 million. Given the type of guarantees usable by PEFCO, customer financing of this type of export is almost entirely dependent on commercial banks and suppliers' credits at existing market rates. A facility especially tailored to the financing requirements of smaller, less well-known businesses and banks could serve the export-expansion program and the national interest. It could also serve the small exporters, those who like many machine tool companies typically write export contracts in the $1 million to $3 million range, that are excluded from Eximbank credits, and that in the environment of the early 1980s are unable to compete with European or Japanese credit terms.

A new financial institution designed to support the financing of exports on short- and medium-term credits at competitive rates would require one or several forms of federal concessions, depending on the degree of foreign subsidized competition. The concession could take the form of selective exemptions from U.S. income taxes for interest payments on borrowings and undistributed profits (GATT commitments would require that such a concession be carefully fashioned), federal guarantees on credit transactions, or exemption from reserve requirements, for example. Such a facility could be constructed on the basis of the existing Eximbank/PEFCO operation, or this could be supplemented by a new foreign-trade bank network chartered specifically to engage in banking operations associated with export finance. Foreign-trade banks have long been part of the commercial banking structures in Europe.

Such an institution might in addition be given authority to buy export paper from commercial banks, package such paper into securities (in the fashion of the Freddie Mac in the field of home mortgages), and resell these securities to individuals and institutions in the private sector. The market for such an institution's securities would be considerably broader than that for the export paper of smaller regional banks, and if, in addition, the new securities were tax free and government guaranteed, the market would be sizable. The availability of such a facility would extend the resources of the commercial banking system and make export finance a more-attractive form of banking activity because even the smaller banks would be able to sell their export paper at a relatively low discount rate to the foreign-trade bank (or enlarged PEFCO facility). Educating medium- and small-scale American business to the opportunities existing outside the United States is widely recognized as essential to long-run, sustained export expansion. Such an institution would facilitate the educational process, as well as serve existing needs for competitive finance.

New Instruments to Finance Exports

Export Bonds

Export bonds, the interest on which would not be subject to income taxes, have been the subject of a variety of suggestions. Such bonds, to be issued by the Eximbank as a means of expanding it resources, have already been mentioned. Other suggestions involving export bonds have entailed the creation of a private-sector issuing facility widely owned by exporters, large and small, that could borrow and lend to exporters both long and short term in small or large amounts. Such bonds, representing the full faith and credit of all associated issuers, would have a ready market even without a government guarantee and would be salable at a lower rate than that available to any one of them singly. The associated issuers could form an entity together that might be a not-for-profit corporation (such as a cooperative) or a profit-making institution (for example, an export bank). The antitrust implications of such an association would have to be explored, but they appear not be insurmountable.

Another variation of the export bond would use the existing authority of municipal and state governments to issue tax-free industrial revenue and development bonds to expand employment and income opportunities within the local jurisdiction. Typically a state or local government will issue a tax-free industrial revenue bond in its own name and make the proceeds available to the selected business in what is essentially a low-interest loan; the issuing authority typically is not liable for interest payments on the bonds.[15] As far as is known, little if any use has been made of industrial revenue bonds for activities aimed primarily or exclusively at the export market, but there is no reason why they should not be so used if they meet the requirements of such issues. The effectiveness of these bonds in generating economic expansion as opposed to simple relocation of industry from one area to another has been the subject of controversy. Certainly the availability of low-cost credit could make the difference between winning an export order and losing it and thus could contribute to a new expansion of economic activity. Probably an important reason they have not been used for purely export operations lies in the degree of foreign competition in low interest rates. The cost saving to the exporter available from such tax-free bonds recently has not been sufficient to meet the competition.

Other variations of export bonds involve not tax-free bonds but a government guarantee—that is, not a tax concession but the creation of a contingent liability by the government. (Guarantees differ from government insurance programs in that they are unconditional in their coverage.) Their use, for example, in a program of cofinancing of U.S. exports to the developing countries by private industry and the government would involve a loan made by a private U.S. lender, guaranteed by the U.S. government, to a developing country receiving assistance from AID, the private loan being matched by an AID loan to the same borrower. Such cofinancing operations are used extensively by other countries competing with U.S. exporters of capital goods. They have the advantage of extending the resources of the aid agencies by drawing on the resources of the private sector and are not likely to represent a cost to the U.S. Treasury.

Long-term bonds as a form of borrowing, even tax-free and government-guaranteed long-term bonds, fell out of investor favor at the end of the 1970s. In fact, the market for long-term bonds has shrunk to such a degree that serious questions have arisen about whether it will ever revive in the United States. The disfavor is the direct result of the shock of volatile interest rates soaring to unprecedented heights, the prime rate having reached 20 percent by 1981 and long-term government bonds backed by the full faith and credit of the United States yielding about 15 percent.

In the past the market has typically valued the tax-free feature of long-term bonds at about 3 percentage points. This spread is, of course, a significant advantage and especially to borrowers of large amounts for a long term, but it is not competitive with foreign subsidies of more than twice that amount. During the first half of 1981, high-grade U.S. municipal bonds yielded over 10 percent while the international arrangement on export credits permitted long-term loans at 7.5 to 8 percent.

As long as investors remain disillusioned about long-term bonds, it is more realistic to think about export bonds of only medium-term maturities (for example, five years). This implies that competitive long-term export finance is likely to be available only from the Eximbank in periods of maximum interest rates and high foreign subsidies. During periods of more-moderate market rates of interest, the private banking sector will require lesser amounts of government support to cope adequately with subsidized competition, and tax-free or government-guaranteed bonds would be more effective as a source of competitive finance.

A variation of the export bond especially tailored to the requirements of the aircraft industry is the international equipment trust certificate (IETC). This is an adaptation of the equipment-trust certificate that has been widely used to finance sales to domestic buyers of such capital goods as ships, rail cars, and aircraft. The adaptation involves a government guarantee of the loan that would cover all commercial and political risks. The government (Eximbank) guarantee is required to extend the market for the certificates to such major private sources of long-term funds as insurance companies, which operate under the "basket rule" prohibiting investment in foreign obligation beyond 2 percent of their total portfolios.[16] The guarantee effectively "domesticates" the obligation. The guarantee would also make the IETCs more attractive to banks and other institutions not so constrained. The certificates would be fashioned to meet the needs of all parties involved: the lenders (banks, insurance companies, pension funds), which establish the trust owning the aircraft, the trust being the lessor; the purchaser, which is the borrower (the airline) and also the lessee; the aircraft manufacturer (the seller); and Eximbank, the guarantor. The trust would own the equipment involved for the benefit of the lenders in the event of bankruptcy; the airline would obtain the tax and depreciation benefits of ownership. The loan would be twelve to eighteen years, reflecting the normal commercial life of the aircraft and could be at a fixed or fluctuating rate or a combination of rates.

As is true of the other variations of export bonds, the IETC would by itself provide export finance at competitive rates only during intervals when export finance is less highly subsidized abroad. If, however, an international agreement among the governments of aircraft-producing countries could be concluded, whereby the counterparts to Eximbank abroad—Export Credit Guarantee Department (ECGD) in Britain, Compagnie Francais d'Assurance pour le Commerce Exterieur (COFACE) in France, for example—were to guarantee the use of IETCs for their own exports of aircraft and to ensure that this would be the only form of government subsidy to export finance for aircraft, a significant part of the practice of predatory export finance would be removed. If Eximbank resources were no longer required by U.S. aircraft exporters because of the availability of competitive financing from the private sector, the bank's ability to serve other exporters would be greatly enhanced.

How willing other OECD governments might be to undertake such an agreement is difficult to judge in advance. Long-term loans disappeared almost completely from European money markets after World War II, a consequence of recurring bouts of inflation and volatile interest rates. How large the private European market would be for IETCs of twelve to eighteen years maturity, even with an adjustable "fixed" rate of interest, can be determined only by testing. There is, however, no reason why IETCs— guaranteed by the European producers of airbus, say, for the export of that aircraft—could not be marketed in the United States where the reluctance of lenders to undertake long-term commitments has been lower than in Europe. U.S. market conditions would determine the rate at which they might be marketable here and thus would effectively ration credit in periods of tightness. A reciprocity clause in an international agreement could make the European and Japanese markets and currency financing available to U.S. issuers of IETCs (although markets like those for the Swiss franc or Japanese yen are very thin). The opportunity to use export-financing instruments of maturities longer than ten years would certainly be attractive to European aircraft exports.

Tax Benefits

An innovative use of the tax system to support export finance by the private sector that is competitive with foreign financing practices, of minimum cost to the U.S. Treasury, and provides the flexibility necessary to cope with changing competitive conditions and interest-rate levels is one that would encourage U.S. exporters to bid on foreign contracts regardless of the availability of foreign export-finance subsidies. Where the latter is a determining factor in the choice of supplier, the U.S. lender would be able to offer a matching or competitive interest rate knowing that, if the contract were then awarded to the U.S. supplier, all interest cost above the competitive rate would be the subject of a direct tax credit. The tax credit could be used either by the commercial bank providing the financing or by the supplier and would be computed on the basis of a monthly average of rates on six-month U.S. Treasury bills plus the interest-rate spread of the bank. (The difference between this composite and the competitive rate would determine the export credit for each year of the life of the export loan.[17]) The Eximbank could verify the fact of the foreign subsidy by means of a certificate that would provide the documentation necessary for the tax credit.

One advantage of such a mechanism is that it would be available to all exporters, small and large. Export contracts of less than $5 million currently are almost totally dependent on the private market; only the discount-credit program of the Eximbank is available to them, and that is limited in size and frequently oversubscribed. This source of potential U.S. exports is currently the stepchild of the U.S. export community.

Such a mechanism would be hightly flexible in operation. As U.S. market rates of interest decline, the amount of the tax credit on outstanding export loans would fall. As foreign subsidies ebb and flow, the amount of the tax credit available to new export contracts would fall and rise accordingly. In addition, the potential loss to the Treasury is minimized and might frequently be negative (that is, result in a net gain). The loss to the Treasury would be the difference between the incremental tax receipt that is the result of the extra income the U.S. exporter earns from the export, which would be earned only if the exporter could offer competitive financing, and the aggregate of tax credits granted over the life of the loan.

5 Emerging Trends

In addition to proposals concerned with government support for export finance, a number of suggestions are being discussed that involve public institutions in support of exports generally. The controversial Domestic International Sales Corporation (DISC), a special type of U.S. corporation established in 1971 for business engaged in export sales, provides a tax benefit for exports. Over the years, changes in basic law increased the complexities and ambiguities of its implementation, and these together with challenges as to its compliance with the GATT have been the source of many suggestions for revising the DISC program. These range from a proposal to exempt from U.S. taxation all export-related income to changing the DISC into a world trade corporation that would be established outside the United States to sell exports and would not be subject to any U.S. taxes. The DISC or proposed variants provide support for exports in general, not for export finance. The same is true of proposals like the creation of trading companies or an expansion of the Overseas Private Investment Corporation. Nonetheless, as is true with government support for R&D, all support affects the bottom line and thus contributes to the ability of U.S. exporters to meet foreign subsidized credits for finance.

Especially encouraging is the intitiative being undertaken by the United States to extend the GATT beyond concern with international trade in commodities to include services trade as well. There is much groundwork to be done before a formal initiative can be launched because so little is known about the facts of international trade in services. The vast data-collection efforts of the U.S. government do not encompass exports of services; estimates of even the aggregate of these exports are just that—subjective estimates based on partial and very incomplete knowledge about the volume of sales to foreigners of engineering and managerial services; banking, brokerage, insurance, and other financial services; planning, statistical, accounting, and executive services; transportation, forwarding, and other freight services; and tourist and other such personal services.

We do know, however, that services in general are one of the most dynamic areas of our economy; they account for at least one-quarter of U.S. exports, employ more than 65 percent of the U.S. nonagricultural work force, and account for about two-thirds of U.S. GNP. In some of these service industries, the comparative advantage of the United States—at least as it has existed in the past—is clear. The present trend of the U.S. position in world services markets is less clear. Given the importance of services in the U.S. economy and in U.S. exports, however, it is important that policies aimed at creating an environment favorable to exports should explicitly include exports of certain service items. The full list of services in which the United States has a clear comparative advantage requires considerable research.

6 Conclusion

The United States is the only nation in which it is necessary to justify exports; in every other country the importance of exports is self-evident and generally accepted. In every other country exports are accorded top priority in national policy; in fashioning domestic economic policy the first concern is its impact on exports. In administering foreign policy, the first concern of foreign service officers abroad, from the country's ambassador on down, is the furtherance of exports. Foreign-aid programs are generally more popular abroad (or less unpopular) because they are perceived as an instrument of export expansion. Geopolitical and defense strategy is pressed with an eye always cocked toward export markets.

The contrast with the United States could hardly be greater. Not only are U.S. exports not accorded priority in domestic or foreign policy, they are actually regarded as subordinate to domestic production in importance. Exports are clearly perceived as expendable whenever export restraint is used as an instrument of foreign policy or is the inevitable consequence of national policy, as was evidenced with increasing frequency during the 1970s. Nothing is more revealing of the warped U.S. perception than the allegation by U.S. government officials that "exports add no more to GNP than production for domestic consumption."[1] In every other country such a statement would evoke a gasp of incredulity from the majority of the electorate. In the United States it went unchallenged. Similarly the failure of the Reagan administration's budget proposals to differentiate between those affecting domestic production and those affecting exports reflects the same inattention to priorities. Despite an expressed goal of reinvigorating the U.S. economy, a failure to recognize the role of foreign trade in influencing the structure of the domestic economy and the contribution of foreign trade to the productivity of U.S. capital, labor, and management will condemn these efforts if not to failure, then to less than maximum effectiveness.

There are, fortunately, signs that these faulted perceptions are changing, in the legislative branch more so than in the executive branch. The formation of an Export Caucus and an Export Task Force in the Senate and House of Representatives bespeaks an awakening awareness of the importance of exports to U.S. national security as well as to U.S. economic health and vitality. The new awareness, it is hoped, will spread quickly.

The reasons for the importance of exports have been recognized by economists since Adam Smith. More recently political scientists and international-affairs specialists have come to recognize the political and strategic importance of exports to a country's national security. The far greater awareness of the economic importance of exports that exists elsewhere is traceable to the limited size of national markets and the importance to a number of industries of economies of scale. To achieve the economies resulting from long production runs, sales outside the limited domestic market are necessary. Similar limitations do not exist in comparable U.S. industries.

The economic benefits of exports are not confined to those that are the consequence of large-scale production, however. Exports of those goods and services that are highly valued by consumers around the world and that can be produced by one country, the United States, for example, more efficiently than it produces other goods tend to raise the nation's productivity. In freely competitive world markets, exporting the products in which the country is most efficient (whether from large-scale industries or small) and importing the goods in which it is less efficient will cause its labor, capital, and management to be used most productively. Any diversion of resources from the more-efficient to the less-efficient uses will lower national productivity. These productivity benefits exist independently of economies of larger production runs. This point is especially relevant for the U.S. economy where the high productivity of many of its service sectors implies large productivity benefits from the exports of such service items as data communication, computer software, and industrial engineering.

The productivity benefits are not the only advantages of exports. A strong export performance enhances the influence and prestige of the nation in all international dealings, causing its diplomats to be listened to seriously, its political and geopolitical initiatives to be more effective, and generally giving the country more clout in the world arena. The prime examples of such enhanced international influence stemming from exports are Germany and Japan. A strong export performance enhances the country's national-security position in the world in part because it is accompanied by a strong foreign-exchange position for its currency. The symbol of a strong currency carries with it a degree of power and influence in the rest of the world that is only poorly recognized in the United States. This power and influence extends to political and military affairs as well as economic.

In the United States we identify our most-efficient industries as our growth industries. They are high-growth industries because consumers at home and abroad value their products highly and demand them in expanding volume. Because of this country's size and its history of support for R&D, the most-efficient industries in the United States (on a world scale) are those that are technologically most advanced. These have produced new products, services, or methods that have found a ready and expanding market at home and abroad. Because of their high growth, output per unit of input (per unit of labor, capital, and management) has been high. This ratio is the economic manifestation of efficiency.

The very success of the growth industries in the United States has caused them to be copied abroad. Such replication would follow, eventually, in the normal course of the product cycle in a world of free competitive markets without government intervention. In fact, however, world markets have been so highly competitive and expanding exports have been so important to Europe and Japan since 1973 (because of unemployment at home and the mushrooming of their oil import bill) that other governments have intervened with direct and indirect subsidies. As a result the replication abroad of U.S. growth industries has caused U.S. exports to be less than they would have been without foreign-government intervention. Such a foreshortening of the flow of U.S. exports has been accompanied by a diversion of U.S. labor and capital away from the more-efficient growth industries into the less-efficient, less-productive domestic industries.

To avoid the depressing effect on U.S. productivity that is the result of foreign-government interference in the market mechanism, the best solution for the United States would be an elimination of foreign-government interference. Such a move is not within the control of the United States, and all of economic history suggests that a policy of government support for exports in some form will never be totally abandoned by U.S. competitors. A prudent course of action, admittedly second best, for the United States requires recognition of such facts of global economic life.

The second-best solution is a policy of countersubsidies by the United States, which would match the export subsidies provided by foreign governments to their replication of industries in which the United States has a clear comparative advantage. Such countersubsidies would neutralize the distorting effects on U.S. resource allocation of foreign-government intervention in the world market mechanism. Both prudence and equity would require that such a program be conceived for the long term and be flexible, capable of fluctuating with the level of foreign subsidies.

A program combining U.S. government support for R&D and for export finance could be effectively fashioned for such flexibility. Much of the institutional foundation for such a program is already in place. Government support for basic research in general and in such areas as defense and public health is in the national interest. Although such support does not benefit exports directly, eventual adaptations in the civilian private sector have the potential of giving a strong boost to exports in the future. Subsidies to R&D, which are justifiable quite apart from what foreign competitors may be doing, can serve as a safety net to counter low-level foreign subsidies to competing industries abroad. For those periods when foreign subsidies rise precipitously, as they recently have, additional support should be available to neutralize their more seriously distorting effects.

Such additional subsidies could take the form of further support for R&D or for export finance. Such a form of government support is appropriate, especially for periods such as the present when foreign subsidies to export credits are grossly distorting the world market mechanism. Subsidies to export finance require that the U.S. Congress decide whether the Eximbank is to be a self-supporting institution or one that meets foreign competition. In periods of heavy foreign subsidies to export finance, the bank cannot do both. Then a decision not to meet foreign competition is in fact a decision to reduce the productivity of U.S. labor and capital.

It is important to be clear about what the government should not attempt to do in support of exports. The government should attempt to work with the market mechanism, not contrary to it. This implies arrangements only to counter the market-distorting policies of other sovereign governments and not to go beyond such neutralizing acts. It means policies aimed at achieving a composition and volume of exports as close as possible to that which would have in fact occurred had not foreign governments undertaken market-distorting policies. It is in part a reactive policy, not an active one, but only in part.

Government policy toward exports and R&D should be active in the limited sense of providing a total environment favorable to such activity. In the case of exports this means government policies that recognize the importance of exports to national productivity and structural growth and means therefore that any reindustrialization program must involve the establishment of priorities for reindustrialization among U.S. industries on the basis of their comparative advantage in the world marketplace. In the case of R&D, it involves government support for those types of R&D activity that the private sector by itself is likely to ignore—basic research and national-security-oriented R&D. Government support for exports and for R&D does not mean a determination by the U.S. government of which industries are to be the growth industries of the future. It means, rather, encouraging the market mechanism to greater alacrity in making that determination. In the case of export finance it means mandating the Eximbank to meet foreign competition as its first and primary goal, with the goal of being self-supporting only secondary. Finally, government policy requires an enduring consensus between the public and private sectors about the importance of exports and an institutional basis for constructing and supporting such a consensus.

In a period when the productivity of the U.S. economy is already depressed seriously by the adverse shift in its terms of trade resulting from unprecedented oil prices, it is important that productivity not be further injured by structural maladjustments induced by the sovereign acts of foreign governments. Such injurious effects can be neutralized by a program of countersubsidies. They can also be countered by a vibrant R&D performance that generates a continuing stream of commercially significant innovations. Successful R&D activity implies a sustained world demand for the exports of the country, an internationally strong currency, and enhanced power and prestige in the international arena.[2]

Endnotes

Preface

1. Before the U.S. House of Representatives, Committee on Banking, Finance, and Urban Affairs, Subcommittee on International Trade Investment and Monetary Policy, Hearings, April 28, 1981.

Chapter 1

1. It was only during the Tokyo Round of Multilateral Trade Negotiations (1979) that the United States finally agreed to abandon the American selling price basis of import valuation on benzenoid chemicals, a means introduced during World War I of protecting the then-infant chemical industry.

2. Indirect subsidies can exist in almost infinite variety. Government procurement that more than covers the cost of production, including a "normal" profit, involves an element of subsidy. Marketing efforts abroad by an embassy's personnel in favor of that country's exports involve a hidden subsidy, as do tax and credit policies that favor exports over production for the domestic market. The United States is not totally innocent of such practices. U.S. military procurement and defense R&D probably often involve a subsidy element, for example. Most competent U.S. observers agree, however, that total U.S. government support for exports (whatever its total) is significantly smaller than that of several of its competitors.

3. Much of this research has been done at the Harvard Business School under the direction of Raymond Vernon. See Raymond Vernon, "International Investment and International Trade in the Product Cycle," *Quarterly Journal of Economics* (May 1966); see also Raymond F. Mikesell and Mark G. Farah, *U.S. Export Competitiveness in Manufactures in Third World Markets,* Significant Issue Series, Vol. 2, No. 9 (Washington, D.C.: Georgetown University Center for Strategic and International Studies, 1980). Edwin Mansfield, "International Technology Transfer: Notes, Benefits, Costs, and Public Policy" (paper presented at the December 1981 annual meeting of the American Economic Association), notes the accelerated rate at which U.S. firms now (1981) begin overseas production after the first U.S. introduction of a new product.

91

4. The current excess capacity of the steel industry worldwide is an extreme example of the impact of government subsidies on investment. In addition, a number of industry observers believe that the world will suffer excess capacity in commercial aircraft for some years.

5. Foreign-government policies were more favorable to foreign exporters than were U.S. government policies toward U.S. exporters not only because of foreign-government support but increasingly through the 1970s because of U.S. government disincentives toward U.S. exports. It is important to note that the total removal of U.S. government disincentives toward exports would not neutralize the impact of government interference on U.S. exports; there would still remain the more-generous treatment of foreign exporters by their governments.

6. The term *Silicon Valley,* for example, was coined to apply to that part of California where the microchip industry (one of great technological vibrancy) is located.

7. Penelope Hartland-Thunberg, *Has the U.S. Export Problem Been Solved?* Significant Issue Series, Vol. 3, No. 1 (Washington, D.C.: Georgetown University Center for Strategic and International Studies, 1981).

8. See, for example, Lawrence G. Franko and Sherry Stephenson, *French Export Behavior in Third World Markets,* Significant Issue Series, Vol. 2, No. 6 (Washington, D.C.: Georgetown University Center for Strategic and International Studies, 1980); and Eleanor M. Hadley, *Japan's Export Competitiveness in Third World Markets,* Significant Issue Series, Vol. 3, No. 2 (Washington, D.C.: Georgetown University Center for Strategic and International Studies, 1981). See also "France Flaunts New Economic Muscle," *Fortune,* May 4, 1981; "Dutch Cabinet Offers $320 million to Finance Development of Plane," *Wall Street Journal,* May 18, 1981; W. Stephen Piper, *U.S. International Competitiveness: The Aerospace Industry,* testimony before U.S. House of Representatives, Committee on Foreign Affairs, Subcommittee on International Economic Policy and Trade, March 19, 1981; Kenneth Walters and Joseph Monsen, "State-owned Business Abroad: New Competitive Threat," *Harvard Business Review* (March–April 1979).

9. See, for example, *Financial Times* (London) *World Business Weekly,* August 18, 1980, p. 26; "Japan Plant Makers Pin Their Hopes on Southeast Asia: Exporters Use Government Aid, New Strategy in Bid to Offset Slumping Orders Elsewhere," *Asian Wall Street Journal,* May 18, 1981.

10. Harald B. Malmgren, *Changing Forms of World Competition and World Trade Rules,* Significant Issue Series, Vol. 3, No. 3, (Washington, D.C.: Georgetown University Center for Strategic and International Studies, 1981).

11. See, for example, Mikesell and Farah, *U.S. Export Competitiveness,* pp. 96–97; *Aviation Week and Space Technology,* March 9, 1981, pp. 173; Robert Hayes and William Abernathy, "Managing Our Way to Economic Decline," *Harvard Business Review* (July–August 1980); M. Nishimizur and Dale W. Jorgensen, "U.S. and Japanese Economic Growth, 1952–74: An International Comparison," *Economic Journal* (December 1978). There is no satisfactory way of measuring the effectiveness of R&D activities. The indexes usually cited—share of GNP devoted to R&D, new patents applied for, relative importance of scientists and engineers in the labor force—all point to a decline in the relative position of the United States. At the start of the 1980s the United States had a $30 billion surplus in trade in high-technology goods; in 1960 the U.S. share of world trade in high-technology goods was 30 percent, while two decades later that share was down to 20 percent. Statement of Lionel H. Olmer, undersecretary of commerce for international trade, before U.S. House of Representatives, Ways and Means Committee, Trade Subcommittee, November 3, 1981.

12. The theory rests upon a logically elegant mathematical proof for the general case. See R.G. Lipsey and R.K. Lancaster, "The General Theory of Second Best," *Review of Economic Studies* 24 (1956–1957).

13. Congressional Budget Office, "The Benefits and Costs of the Export-Import Bank Loan Subsidy Program," photocopied (March 1981). With the exception of chapters 4 and 6, this study implicitly assumes no foreign subsidies.

14. It is in the nature of the second-best alternative that the option that is judged to be the second best cannot be proved for the general case. It cannot be proved unequivocally that the second-best choice for the United States in the 1980s is that of neutralizing foreign subsidies in industries in which the United States has a clear comparative advantage. Even if there were no data problems and one could get any and all information one wanted, an unequivocal proof still would not be possible. This is basically because the argument is a categorical negative: it claims there is no other conceivable option possible that would yield a better solution (excluding, of course, the first best). With no data problems, one could examine an infinite number of other alternatives and prove that none of them is as favorable as the stated second best, but still it would not be possible to prove that there is not yet another (infinity-plus-one) alternative that is better. In brief, all that can be done is to state that an examination of the available facts creates the strong presumption that the true second-best choice lies in such-and-such a policy. This is the reason for the conditional statement: "The specifics of the U.S. in the world economy of the 1980s *strongly suggest* that the second-best policy for the United States. . . ."

15. From testimony of T.A. Wilson, chairman Boeing Company,

before U.S. House of Representatives, Committee on Banking, Finance and Urban Affairs, Subcommittee on International Trade, Investment and Monetary Policy, March 5, 1981.

16. Officials of the Eximbank were very helpful in the elaboration of the example, especially James Cruse, vice-president for policy analysis.

17. This definition and the subsequent discussion is adopted from Penelope Hartland-Thunberg, "U.S. Third World Policy and National Interests," testimony before U.S. Senate, Committee on Foreign Relations, Subcommittee on International Economic Policy, February 25, 27, 1981, pp. 205–218; and from Penelope Hartland-Thunberg, *The Political and Strategic Importance of Exports,* Significant Issue Series, Vol. 1, No. 3 (Washington, D.C.: Georgetown University Center for Strategic and International Studies, 1979).

18. *New York Times,* February 11, 1981.

19. *Washington Post,* March 13 and November 12, 1978.

20. Mikesell and Farah, *U.S. Export Competitiveness,* p. 7.

21. Ibid.

22. For a more-complete treatment of this subject, see Hartland-Thunberg, *U.S Third World Policy.*

Chapter 2

1. Cf. Michael Noelke and Robert Taylor, *EEC Protectionism: Present Practice and Future Trends* (Brussels: European Research Associates, 1981). Robert A. Flammang, *U.S. Programs That Impede U.S. Export Competitiveness: The Regulatory Environment,* Significant Issues Series, Vol. 2, No. 3 (Washington, D.C.: Georgetown University Center for Strategic and International Studies, 1980); Simon Serfaty, *The United States, Western Europe, and the Third World: Allies and Adversaries,* Significant Issues Series, Vol. 2, No. 4 (Washington, D.C.: Georgetown University Center for Strategic and International Studies, 1980).

2. "Third World Plans Export Credit System," *Financial Times* (London), July 2, 1981.

3. In this book the term *subsidies* is always to be understood in the broadest sense to include not only direct subsidies (cash payments by the government) but also indirect subsidies (such as concessions or benefits conferred by the government in the form of taxes, guarantees, and such).

4. In attempting to justify their own subsidies, competitors make much of the fact that U.S. growth industries have received government subsidies in this fashion. It is convenient for them to ignore the higher tax burden that the U.S. defense effort imposes on U.S. industry. Because they benefit both from U.S. defense capabilities and the civilian adaptations of defense-generated technology, their allegations that they are justified in their own subsidies to high technology industries are disingenuous.

5. It would take an immense team of accountants, lawyers, economists, and engineers to compute the amount of government subsidy, income attributable to it, and overall net gain to the government in taxes after X years for any single government-supported technological advance. It is not intuitively clear that the results of such an effort would be worth its cost.

6. J. Fred Bucy, "Controlling Exports of Technology," *International Security* (Winter 1981).

7. David Ford and Chris Ryan, "Taking Technology to Market," *Harvard Business Review* (March–April 1981).

Chapter 3

1. George Keyworth, "Science and Technology Policy—What's Ahead?" at the American Association for the Advancement of Science (AAAS) Colloquium on R&D, Washington, D.C., June 25, 1981.

2. OECD, *Technical Change and Economic Policy* (Paris: OECD, 1980). Member countries of OECD are Australia, Austria, Belgium, Canada, Denmark, Finland, France, Federal Republic of Germany, Greece, Iceland, Ireland, Italy, Japan, Luxembourg, Netherlands, New Zealand, Norway, Portugal, Spain, Sweden, Switzerland, Turkey, United Kingdom, and the United States.

3. Malcolm Baldrige, testimony before U.S. Senate, Interstate and Foreign Commerce Committee, May 26, 1981.

4. Robert H. Hayes and William J. Abernathy, "Managing Our Way to Decline," *Harvard Business Review* (July–August 1980).

5. Office of Management and Budget, *A Program for Economic Recovery* (February 1981).

6. Elmer Staats, luncheon address before the AAAS Colloquium on R&D, June 25, 1981.

7. OECD, *Technical Change and Economic Policy.*

8. OECD, *Science Resources Newsletter No. 5* (Summer 1980). These data cover only OECD members. Comparable data for other countries are not available.

9. The Frascati Manual was originally published in 1976 and is currently being revised. Its formal title is *The Measurement of Scientific and Technical Activities: Proposed Standard Practice for Surveys of Research and Experimental Developments* (Paris: OECD, 1976).

10. Research and development in the Frascati Manual covers three activities: basic research to acquire new knowledge of underlying foundations of phenomena and observable facts; applied research to acquire new knowledge directed at a specific practical objective; and experimental development and systematic work to produce new materials, products, or devices, to install new processes, systems, and services, or to improve sub-

stantially those already produced or installed. Excluded from data collection are such R&D-related activities as education and training, testing and standardization, information distribution, extension and advisory services, patent and license administration, commercial and marketing innovation, and production and distribution beyond the pilot plant. Five national sectors are covered: business enterprises and nonprofit and research institutes; central, provincial, and municipal governments; higher education; international and foreign institutions; and philanthropical organizations.

11. Adding our estimates of U.K. R&D to the OECD data would alter these ratios and show the United States performing 46 percent of all R&D and 49 percent of industrial R&D of the OECD countries.

12. U.S. Department of Commerce, *Schedule E, Exports by Commodity* (1980).

13. U.S. Department of Commerce, *U.S. General Imports Schedule A* (1980). The estimate in the text is a minimum, and lower than that of Under Secretary Olmer (see note 11) probably because of differences in coverage.

14. No attempt is made here to address the drag on earnings from high-technology exports due to U.S. government laws and regulations, like the taxation of Americans abroad, antiboycott and antitrust legislation, and other such U.S. programs that impede U.S. export competitiveness. See, for example, Flammang, *U.S. Programs.*

15. OECD, *Science Resources Newsletter No. 5.*

16. Several OECD internal studies have been conducted on the technical measurement of commercial effectiveness of R&D. This paragraph draws heavily on that analysis.

17. OECD, *Science Resources Newsletter No. 5.*

18. See also C.T. Hill and J.M. Utterback, *Technological Innovation for a Dynamic Economy* (New York: Pergamon, 1979), for a lengthy discussion of evidence showing that U.S. outlays for R&D may have a weaker economic impact than others. Some other measurements of commercial effectiveness, such as the ratios of corporate R&D to corporate earning rates, might show the United States more favorably compared to other nations. These other measurements have some degree of validity; nevertheless the measurements that we have seen presented in a time series show a declining trend for U.S. commercial effectiveness.

19. Bruno O. Weinschel, *R&D in the FY 1982 Budget: Assessing the Impacts,* AAAS Colloquium, June 25, 1981.

20. OECD, *Technical Change and Economic Policy.*

21. *Research and Development Report VI* (Washington, D.C.: American Association for the Advancement of Science, 1981).

22. OECD, *Technical Change and Economic Policy.*

23. *Science,* August 21, 1981, pp. 844–845.

24. *Economist,* March 14, 1981.

25. Quoted in *Computer World,* May 25, 1981.

26. OECD, *Technical Change and Economic Policy.*

27. OECD, *Small and Medium Firms and Technical Change* (May 18, 1981).

28. *Economist,* March 14, 1981.

29. Ibid., June 13, 1981.

30. Daniel S. Greenberg, "Our Indolent Pursuit of Foreign Technology," *Washington Post,* April 11, 1978.

31. Department of Commerce, *U.S. Semi-Conductor Industry* (Washington, D.C.: Government Printing Office, 1980).

32. *Japan* (Washington, D.C.: Science and Government Report, Inc., 1979).

33. *Economist,* July 18, 1981.

34. Japan Management Association, Future Trends in the Use of Microcomputers and Their Use in Japan, trans. U.S. Department of State, Washington, D.C., 1980.

35. The definition of *robot* in Japan covers a wider variety of machines than in the United States.

36. *Nihon Keizai Shimbun* (Tokyo), reprinted in *World Press Review* (August 1981).

37. W. Michael Blumenthal, Keynote address before the National Computer Conference, Chicago, May 6, 1981.

38. O.H. Ganley and G.D. Ganley, "The U.S. and Its Communication and Information Resources: International Implications," manuscript, (Cambridge: Harvard University Center for Information Policy Research, 1981).

39. *Financial Times* (London), May 18, 1981.

40. *Gulf Mirror* (Bahrein), from *World Press Review* (August 1981).

41. *Economist,* February 28, 1981.

42. *InterMedia* (London: Institute for Communications, January 1981).

43. Ganley and Ganley, *U.S. and Its Communication and Information Resources.*

44. Ibid.

45. *Economist,* May 30, 1981.

46. Ibid. Fuel cost estimate is from the Boeing Company.

47. *Economist,* June 27, 1981.

48. *Financial Times* (London), January 25, 1981.

49. P.A.J. Tindemans, Director General, Ministry for Science and Research, Netherlands, "Innovation Policy: Trends and Perspectives," mimeographed (Paris: OECD, December 1980).

50. T. Gaudin, Ministry of Industry, France, "Innovations Policy: Proceedings," mimeographed (Paris: OECD, December 1980).

51. *Journal of Commerce,* August 31, 1981.

52. A. Carocciolo, Universite Pro Deo, "Innovations Policy: Proceedings," mimeographed (Paris: OECD, 1980).

53. OECD, "Innovations Policy: Proceedings," 1980.

54. OECD, *Science Resources Newsletter No. 5.*

55. *Japan* (Washington, D.C.: Science and Government Report, Inc., 1979).

56. Ibid.

57. S. Sonoyama, *Japanese Innovation Policy* (Paris: OECD, 1980).

58. *Japan* (Washington, D.C.: Science and Government Report, Inc., 1979).

59. Sonoyama, *Japanese Innovation Policy.*

60. Ibid.

61. *Germany* (Washington, D.C.: Science and Government Report, Inc., 1979).

62. *Economist,* April 11, 1981.

63. *Software AG Prospectus,* June 8, 1981.

64. *France* (Washington, D.C.: Science and Government Report, Inc., 1979).

65. Judith Allen, ed., "France," *Guide to World Science,* vol. 2 (Washington, D.C.: 1979).

66. Simon Nora and Alain Minc, *Report on the Computerization of Society* (Cambridge: MIT Press, 1980).

67. Andre Giraud, Minister of Industry, Keynote address at OECD Conference, October 6, 1980.

68. Gaudin, "Innovations Policy."

69. OECD, "Inventory of Innovation Policies," mimeo. Paris, 1981.

70. J. Fred Bucy, "Controlling Exports of Technology," *International Security* (Winter 1981).

71. Office of the White House Press Secretary, "The President's Industrial Innovation Incentives," (October 31, 1979). See also Jordan Baruch, *The U.S. Domestic Policy Review of Industrial Innovation* (Washington, D.C.: Department of Commerce, June 1980).

72. Murray Weidenbaum, "Private Sector, Research and Development, and the President's Program," paper presented at the AAAS Colloquium on R&D, June 25, 1981.

73. C. Jackson Grayson, *Duns Review* (July 1979):8.

Chapter 4

1. The break-even point depends on the life of the loan and its time pattern. With semiannual servicing (fully amortized with even semiannual

repayments), the average life of a five-year-loan is 33 months (2.75 years); then each 1 percent of interest differential amounts to 2.75 percent of the total sum being financed. Thus, 7 percent divided by 2.75 is 2.55; subtracting 2.55 from 20 percent yields 17.5 percent.

2. The following discussion summarizing the official export-credit systems of the major trading countries draws heavily on Joan Pearce, *Subsidized Export Credit,* Chatham House Papers no. 8 (London: Royal Institute of International Affairs, 1981); articles in the International Monetary Fund *Survey* (March 15, June 7, July 5, 1976; January 24, February 21, March 7, 1977; July 3, 1978; November 26, 1979) by Albert C. Cizauskas; Export-Import Bank of the United States, *Report to the U.S. Congress on Export Credit Competition and the Export-Import Bank of the U.S.,* assorted annual issues; Albert C. Cizauskas, *Changing Nature of Export Credit Financing and Its Implications for Developing Countries,* World Bank Staff Working Paper No. 409 (Washington, D.C.: World Bank, 1980).

3. For example, short-term rates in the United States declined by 1,000 basis points in the first half of 1980, then rose by 1,200 basis points in the second half of the same year. Morgan Guaranty Survey, September 1981.

4. *Euromoney* (July 1981):161.

5. Statement of Mark E. Leland, assistant secretary of treasury for international affairs, before U.S. House of Representatives, Committee on Ways and Means, Subcommittee on International Trade, November 2, 1981.

6. *Selection and Development of a Private Sector Financing Instrument,* report prepared for the U.S. Agency for International Development by Peat, Marwick, Mitchell and Company (September 1979).

7. *Economist,* August 15, 1981, p. 14.

8. John E. Mullen, "Export Promotion: Legal and Structural Limitations on Broad U.S. Commitment," *Law and Policy in International Business* 7 (1979).

9. *To Be Self-Sufficient or Competitive? Eximbank Needs Guidance,* Report to the Congress by the Comptroller General of the United States (Washington, D.C., June 24, 1981).

10. Cf. Wilson E. Schmidt, "Eximbank Subsidies Are Not Essential," *Journal of Commerce,* April 6, 1981; Steven E. Plout, "Export-Import Follies," *Fortune,* August 25, 1980; Robert A. Cornell, deputy assistant secretary of the treasury, before U.S. Senate, Committee on Banking, Housing and Urban Affairs, Subcommittee on International Finance and Monetary Policy, July 20, 1981.

11. For example, Gordon C. Hurlbert (Westinghouse Electric Corporation), Earl Doubet (Caterpillar Tractor Company), T.A. Wilson

(Boeing Company), W. Stephen Piper (Office of U.S. Trade Representative) before U.S. Senate, Committee on Banking, Housing, and Urban Affairs, Subcommittee on International Trade, Investment and Monetary Policy, March 15–19, 1981; "C. Fred Bergsten: Champion of Interdependence," *World Business Weekly,* March 2, 1981; "U.S. Firms Already Cut Back Work as Result of Eximbank Restraints," *Wall Street Journal,* March 31, 1981; "Hard Times for the Eximbank," *International Finance,* April 14, 1980 (Chase Manhattan Bank); Kenneth D. Walters and R. Joseph Monsen, "State-owned Business Abroad: New Competitive Threat," *Harvard Business Review* (March–April 1979).

12. *Financial Times* (London), September 26, 1979.

13. In order for private-sector buyers to benefit from the provision in the Internal Revenue Code (section 243), which makes 85 percent of the dividends received by corporations from their holdings of preferred stock nontaxable, the Eximbank would probably have to be made a purely private corporation rather than a mixed public-private facility.

14. In autumn 1981, Eximbank initiated a special facility in the discount-loan program to benefit small business. For companies whose total sales are less than $25 million annually, the discount-loan facility is available at the direct loan rate, which thus entails some subsidy below the prevailing market rates.

15. U.S. House of Representatives, Subcommittee on Oversight of the Committee on Ways and Means, *Report on Tax-Exempt "Small Issue" Industrial Revenue Bonds,* July 9, 1981.

16. *Federal Reserve Bank of New York Quarterly Review* (Autumn 1981):8.

17. Equating the tax credit to the corporate income tax rate, for example, 48 percent of the subsidy, would eliminate an overcompensation of the lender.

Chapter 6

1. It is gratifying to note that officials of the Treasury Department have dropped this pseudo-homily from their recent congressional testimony, in contrast to their utterances earlier in the year.

2. This summary was presented as testimony given by Penelope Hartland-Thunberg, Senior Fellow, Economic Research, Center for Strategic and International Studies, Georgetown University, before U.S. House of Representatives, Committee on Ways and Means, Subcommittee on Trade, December 15, 1981.

Index

About the Authors

Penelope Hartland-Thunberg is Senior Fellow in Economic Studies at the Georgetown University Center for Strategic and International Studies, Washington D.C. Prior to joining the center in 1974, she was a member of the Board of National Estimates, CIA. Dr. Thunberg has been an economist with the Council of Economic Advisers and in 1965 was appointed by President Johnson to be a member of the U.S. Tariff Commission. She received the Ph.D. from Radcliffe College and holds an honorary LL.D. from Brown University. Her articles have appeared in leading professional journals. She is the author of *Botswana: An African Growth Economy* (1978) and *Trading Blocs, U.S. Exports, and World Trade* (1980).

Morris H. Crawford is head of International Informatics, his computer-communications consulting firm that specializes in analysis of international data communication and high-technology trade. He is currently working on a study to be published April 1982 by the Harvard University Center for Information Policy Research entitled "Competition, Cooperation, and Discord in Information Technology Trade." He completed undergraduate and graduate schooling at the University of Chicago, with major fields in economics and philosophy. He served in the U.S. Foreign Service in Southeast Asia and the Middle East, as well as in Washington. He retired in 1980 after twenty-eight years of government service.